CW00740838

THE COMPLETE GUIDE TO CHIHUAHUAS

David Anderson

LP Media Inc. Publishing

Text copyright © 2019 by LP Media Inc.

All rights reserved.

No part of this book may be reproduced or transmitted in any form or by any means, electronic or mechanical, including photocopying, recording, or by an information storage and retrieval system - except by a reviewer who may quote brief passages in a review to be printed in a magazine or newspaper - without permission in writing from the publisher. For information address LP Media Inc. Publishing, 3178 253rd Ave. NW, Isanti, MN 55040

www.lpmedia.org

Publication Data

David Anderson

The Complete Guide to Chihuahuas ---- First edition.

Summary: "Successfully raising a Chihuahua dog from puppy to old age" --- Provided by publisher.

ISBN: 978-1-09554-484-6

[1. Chihuahuas --- Non-Fiction] I. Title.

This book has been written with the published intent to provide accurate and author- itative information in regard to the subject matter included. While every reasonable pre- caution has been taken in preparation of this book the author and publisher expressly dis- claim responsibility for any errors, omissions, or adverse effects arising from the use or application of the information contained inside. The techniques and suggestions are to be used at the reader's discretion and are not to be considered a substitute for professional veterinary care. If you suspect a medical problem with your dog, consult your veterinarian.

Design by Sorin Rădulescu

First paperback edition, 2019

TABLE OF CONTENTS

CHAPTER 7.
The First Month

CHAPTER 8.
Housetraining

CHAPTER 9.
Socialization and Experience

CHAPTER 10.
Being a Puppy Parent

INTRODUCTION

One of the smallest dogs in the world, Chihuahuas are an intriguing breed. Each dog has to be taken as an individual because their behavior is incredibly unique. The breed comes with one of the widest ranges of personality types, largely formed based on how the Chihuahuas are raised and how much they are socialized in the early days. They also have a wider range in appearance than most breeds, with both the typical short hair and a long-haired version of the breed.

They are easily one of the most polarizing dog breeds because of their small stature and personality. Smaller than many house cats, Chihuahuas do not fit the traditional image of a dog. However, this is what makes them so easy to incorporate into the family. They are incredibly loyal to their family, and tend to be very wary of strangers.

However, not all Chihuahuas are aggressive, and they may end up shivering in an unfamiliar environment. They are very easy companions when you are at home just lounging around. Some of them are also remarkably intelligent, something that the breed is not commonly known for.

With roots firmly planted in Mexico, it is not a surprise that the dog is the national symbol of the country. Many companies have used Chihuahuas as "spokesdogs" for their businesses, with the restaurant Taco Bell being one of the most famous. Obviously, the breed's history is rich and colorful, and it is one of the oldest dog breeds in the Americas.

They do tend to be one of the more difficult breeds to train if you start training when the dog is older, so you could be in for a difficult time if you aren't consistent or if you start when the puppy is almost an adult. Consistency is incredibly important with Chihuahuas. On the other hand, they are one of the easiest breeds to ensure they get adequate exercise. With those little legs moving rapidly to keep up with your legs, you don't have to spend much time walking them. They are also one of the few breeds that experts recommend you keep indoors nearly all of the time. If you train and socialize your Chihuahua from the beginning, you will have an excellent little companion for up to 20 years.

CHAPTER 1.
Fearless, Mischievous Sidekicks – Defining Characteristics

To look at a Chihuahua, you would probably think that there isn't much to see. That is certainly true – a healthy, hardy Chihuahua reaches a maximum weight of 6 pounds. But that little body can pack one heck of a personality.

Few breeds have as diverse a range of temperaments and appearances as the Chihuahua. They come in a large variety of colors and patterns, and include both short and long-haired versions of the breed. The one thing that remains constant is that they are so tiny you can carry them in a large purse – and many celebrities have.

Photo Courtesy of Barbara Pendergrass Rafina Chihuahuas

Descriptions and Defining Characteristics

Easily the most noticeable aspect of the Chihuahua is its size. Their faces are fairly uniform, despite the wide range in color and fur length. With skinny little legs and enormous, wide eyes, there definitely is no mistaking the Chihuahua for any other breed.

Appearance

Looking at a Chihuahua, you may think that the head is about one-third to half of the 5 or 6 pounds of the pup. The head is commonly described as rounded, like an apple. Those large eyes seem to take up a majority of the face, and you definitely feel like you won't get much past your Chihuahua. The only things larger than the eyes are the ears that traditionally stick up like radar dishes, giving the dog a look that makes it seem as though it is on constant high alert. Some Chihuahuas do have ears that flop over, but the majority have the more common straight ears that stand up at attention at every little noise in the home.

Their little bodies look very much like that of a boxer or Great Dane scaled down to a toy size. They can be incredibly muscular, especially since any exercise requires a lot more work on their part to go the same distance as you. Their rapid-paced walking puts speed walkers to shame. The effortless, rapid walk that they do without thinking can give you quite an appreciation for how much they have adapted to become human companions.

Most people imagine the short-haired breed when you say Chihuahua, but there is also a long-haired version. Their bodies are largely the same, but the additional fur makes the long-haired version look a good bit more elegant. The rapid walking makes their hair sway and move in a way reminiscent of the movement of a person's hair in an open convertible. The fur is also a good bit softer.

Their small stature does have the drawback of making them more fragile than most other dog breeds. Children should never be allowed to roughhouse with a Chihuahua as the dog could be easily hurt. They are much more of a lap dog or prankster than a playmate for young children.

Short Hair Chihuahua

11

Temperament

The Chihuahua often seems to ignore it's small stature and can act with the confidence of a much larger dog. The fearless individuals of the breed are incredibly vocal – and they are easily in the majority. This is an ideal apartment breed, but you are going to have your work cut out for you in the early days trying to teach your Chihuahua not to bark at everything. This means they will make great alarms, and it will be difficult for anyone to be near your home without your dog letting you know.

Chihuahuas tend to be either shy or aggressive. They are prone to small-dog syndrome if they are not trained when they are young. It isn't much better if your Chihuahua goes the other way and ends up being afraid of everything.

The long-haired Chihuahuas do tend to have a friendlier disposition, making them more likely to be relaxed at home. This does not mean they won't bark often or that they don't need socialization.

Long Hair Chihuahua

Nearly all Chihuahuas will become incredibly loyal to their family – they love the people and animals in their immediate circle. The breed tends to be wary of strangers, either barking or shivering during introductions to someone new.

They are a decidedly indoor dog, perhaps the most indoor breed of the entire canine kingdom. Most breeders will recommend keeping pee pads or boxes in the home, just like you would with a cat. Unlike other breeds, you can never send your Chihuahua out to do his business and then let the little guy back inside because they are easy prey for predators, including hawks and eagles. This has made the breed far better adapted to staying inside for 23.5 hours out of 24. Even when your dog does go out, you will have to use the leash to protect the little guy. This also explains why they are so protective of their people

– they are just returning the favor for your protection of them. Not that they typically realize just how small they are.

Your Chihuahua will probably walk down the street eyeing everyone and everything and analyzing them to determine how much of a threat they are. Barking will very likely come into play even when the two of you aren't at home, though you can train them to be less vocal on walks if you take some Cheerios with you. It is always entertaining to watch a Chihuahua yapping ferociously at a German Shepherd or Mastiff. Size difference aside, the larger dogs typically look down at the little guy in confusion, or back away, not exactly sure how to react to the small animal. These kinds of encounters will only embolden your Chihuahua, so you will want to train your little puppy to be calmer on walks instead of terrorizing other dogs.

A Distinctive Face and Stature

As mentioned, the head shape of a Chihuahua is incredibly unique. It looks more like the inspiration for an alien head than that of a dog. The large ears help the dog to hear a lot of sounds (though they are not quite as sensitive as working breeds like the Corgi), and they will react. It can be entertaining to just sit and watch

Photo Courtesy of
Joanna Elliker

your Chihuahua try to take in all of the sounds, their large ears twitching and turning at the slightest noise. It will typically be followed by a bout of yapping and running around, unless you train them not to do that.

Probably the most noticeable feature is the eyes. They are large and soulful, giving the Chihuahua a look of either sorrow or alertness that is very difficult to ignore. They definitely know how to use that to their advantage as well. When you are eating, those eyes are going to be begging you to share, and you will have to resist.

The Chihuahua is the smallest dog breed in the world, and that is pretty much the best way to sum them up. They are unbelievably small. This means you are going to need to take an entirely different approach to their care than you would with almost any other breed. They are more fragile than most breeds, and some Chihuahuas are also incredibly intelligent. You have to find the right balance to taking care of them without spoiling them, a feat that isn't as easy as you would imagine.

Photo Courtesy of
Susan Lamb

Wide Range of Potential Personalities

In addition to their various colors of coats, Chihuahuas have a varied personality range. They can be incredibly fierce, constantly yapping at dogs they encounter on walks. Or they can be shy and skittish, something you need to actively work to remedy as much as possible. It is not healthy for them to be constantly scared and shaking. They can also be extremely friendly and bouncy, acting as the life of the party instead of little terrors or cowards.

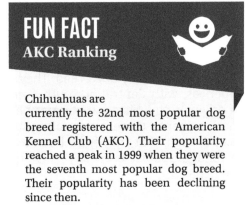

FUN FACT
AKC Ranking

Chihuahuas are currently the 32nd most popular dog breed registered with the American Kennel Club (AKC). Their popularity reached a peak in 1999 when they were the seventh most popular dog breed. Their popularity has been declining since then.

Much of their personality is going to depend on how you train and socialize them. Other aspects of their nature will be directly connected to their parents' temperaments. This is why it is essential to spend a lot of time talking to a breeder if you plan to get a puppy. You want to know what the parents were like so that you will have a much better idea of what kind of temperament your puppy will have. If you rescue a Chihuahua, be prepared for the little guy to take some time to warm up to you before you really get to see the personality. They are wary by nature, and they will be more so when introduced into a new environment.

CHAPTER 2.
Breed History and Characteristics

The Chihuahua may be small, but they have one of the longest histories of any dog breed. They are also a dog that is native to the Americas, with Central or South America being their most likely place of origin. With a history that dates back well before recorded history on the continents, there is a lot of mystery behind their heritage. It is certain, though, that they have been around for much longer than many of today's popular breeds. This is one of the many things that adds to their charm.

Theories of the Chihuahua's Origins

The history of any canine breed that goes back over 1,000 years is going to be shrouded in mystery and legend. The Chihuahua is no different. In fact, it may be even less well understood since the history of the breed has not been well documented. This has led to a lot of speculation, particularly as their popularity never seems to wane. With only a few other notable breeds having such lengthy backstories (like the Corgi and Greyhounds), learning about the Chihuahua can give you a lot more to think about and to research if you are interested. This chapter gives you just a little taste of some of the extensive history and speculation behind this tiny breed of dog.

The Theory of the Techichi

One of the more likely theories about the Chihuahua is that they are a distant descendant of the Techichi. This was a small-framed dog that was a companion of Mesoamerican civilizations. They were likely the traveling companions to Native American tribes in the region now known as Central America and the southern part of North America. The Techichi was a bit larger – it is thought they were between 10 and 20 pounds. Over time, they may have

Photo Courtesy of Rayne Music

evolved to be smaller, losing their long coats in the warm climate. Unlike the Chihuahua, a notorious barker, the Techichi is thought to have been mute. The long-haired Chihuahua does seem to be more similar, if only about half the size of the Techichi, and the fur is similar to what historians believe the Techichi's fur was like.

European Descendants

Some think that the Chihuahua may have originated in Europe in the small country of Malta. Located just south of Italy, Malta has a unique canine breed that is of fairly small stature called the Maltese pocket dog. The unusual undeveloped cranial gap of the Maltese pocket dog is shared with the Chihuahua, something that is not common in dogs (though humans are born with a similar soft spot). The people who believe this theory point to a fresco painted during the Renaissance that included a dog that looks very similar to the Chihuahua. The painting by Sandro Botticelli was completed 10 years before Columbus's first trip across the ocean, so the dog was definitely not influenced by any breeds from the Americas, like the Techichi.

Photo Courtesy of
Barbara Pendergrass
Rafina Chihuahuas

Early Civilizations

Whatever their early parentage, the Chihuahua, or the Techichi, has been around for a long time. The breed has certainly appeared in the art and ruins of many ancient Mesoamerican civilizations.

The Mayans and Toltecs

There is evidence that the Techichi was a part of the Mayan or Toltec civilizations. It is believed that one of these two civilizations first domesticated them. However, it is difficult to determine exactly when the Techichi started living alongside humans because the Mayan civilization ended around 900 AD, as the Toltec civilization was in the early stages of developing. Mayans believed that dogs played a role in the afterlife, which was why dogs were included in burial ceremonies. It is believed that the Techichi were sacrificed and mummified when their people died so that the dog could join their humans in the afterlife. This certainly seems to show a lack of regard for the dog's life according to our thinking today, but dogs played an important part in people's lives during this earlier period. The afterlife would not be complete without their loyal companions.

Dogs were also included in pottery and art, with some pieces that depict dogs believed to be from as long ago as 300 BC. Some of the dogs in the works of art looked very similar to the Chihuahua. One of the most interesting works dates back about 1,200 years in the Mayan ruins and depicts a woman holding a child in one arm and a dog in the other. The dog looks very much like a larger version of the modern-day Chihuahua.

The Aztecs and Arrival of the Europeans

The Toltec civilization was on the decline when the Aztecs began their rise to power. By 1325 AD, the Aztecs had already established the capital where the Spanish conquistadors would visit when they came – Tenochtitlan. The Aztecs had great respect for the crumbling civilization of the Toltecs, so they copied many of the previous civilization's ceremonies. The sacrifice of Techichi was included with the other ceremonies that the Aztecs adopted.

With the arrival of Hernan Cortes, the Techichi seemed to all but disappear, just as the Aztecs did under the conquistadors' attacks. It is likely that the Techichi that survived were bred with other dogs, with the

*Photo Courtesy of
Joanna Elliker*

FUN FACT
Smallest Dog Breed

Chihuahuas are the smallest dog breed, coming in at not more than five inches tall at the shoulder and no heavier than six pounds. That's according to the AKC breed standard, although you may find Chihuahuas outside the show ring that are up to 10 pounds.

Chinese Crested often suggested (they do have a similar appearance to the Chihuahua). This theory relies on the arrival of Chinese explorers reaching the Americas before the Spanish, which is not too far-fetched. The other possible breed that could have bred with the Techichi to make the Chihuahua is the Xoloitzcuintli, more commonly called the Xolo. It is another hairless dog that still roams across Mexico. The Xolo is thought to be several thousand years old. It is also possible that the Chihuahua is the result of breeding with several other dog types not currently known. DNA research is being conducted and has begun to yield some interesting results to help understand just how this breed came to be.

A Unique Mexican History

Chihuahua, Mexico, is a state to the north that borders with Texas and New Mexico. Ironically, Chihuahua is the largest Mexican state, and it is the place where the tiny breed with its name was first identified during the 1800s. Merchants began to make money by selling these unique little dogs to tourists, who could then easily take them home. This is how the breed got its name – the breed was not recognized before this time, so the name of the place was adopted by those explaining where they had acquired their little companions.

Personality to Go AROUND

Chihuahuas are not easy to pin down in terms of personality because, for such an old breed, they come with a lot of variety in their personalities. Unlike breeds like Retrievers and Greyhounds that have fairly predictable personalities, Chihuahuas are notorious for several different types of personalities. Some can be incredibly aggressive, which is itself quite entertaining as they try to take on animals and people much bigger than themselves. Others seem to be scared of their own shadows. They will shake and shiver when you are in a bad mood or when you take them into a different environment. Still others act like incredibly friendly and attentive companions, only looking to enjoy playing with their people.

You can help to mold the personality of your Chihuahua if you start with a puppy. If you get an older dog, you will need to work with an established personality, and it will take some time before the dog warms up to you and the family. However, once the dog does warm up to you, it will be much easier to enjoy whatever personality is already there. It is sometimes more enjoyable to learn about your older dog than to train a puppy from the beginning. And it is often less work.

CHAPTER 3.
The Ideal Home

"Make sure you understand the breed and that the Chihuahua is the right fit for you and your family. Just because they are small and cute doesn't mean they are right for you."

Kathy Golden
Kactus Kathy's Chihuahuas

Photo Courtesy of
Kayleigh Denyer

Because Chihuahuas are such a small dog, these little guys are great in any home, particularly apartments since they don't require any yard at all. Of course, training is absolutely essential to keep your little dog from being either terrified or perpetually vocal if you live in an apartment. They bark – a lot. As long as you properly set up your home, there should not be any significant problems with raising and taking care of your dog. They can be very intelligent, although the intelligent ones do tend to be rather stubborn.

They do all right in heat, but they cannot handle cold. Chihuahuas will start to shiver when they are cold, which is why many people have little sweaters or coats for their dogs. As long as you keep their areas fairly warm, this should not be an issue.

Photo Courtesy of Emma Prince

Best Environment

Smaller homes tend to be best for them, but as long as your Chihuahua can be with you, they really don't care how big the home is. You will need to make sure there are places where your Chihuahua can use the restroom since you won't be able to send them outside on their own because of predators. However, with this small size, having a couple of areas for restroom breaks set up around the home is fairly unobtrusive. The smaller your place, the fewer designated areas you will need.

A Compact Canine for Any Home

A Chihuahua's primary interest is in being near you, like a noon shadow. They will probably follow you around the home, so if you have a larger home, you may not need to go outside for much time at all to exercise your little friend. Even if you have an apartment, it will still be a lot of work for your dog to make it around the place.

With famous people having pictures captured of them carrying their Chihuahuas in their purses or bags, there really is no such thing as too small a space for a Chihuahua, or too large. They are going to stick to you, kind of like a living toy. This is what made them so popular in the early days and why they have kept their popularity. It is not recommended to carry any dog in any kind of bag or carriage as this will spoil the dog. Let your tiny canine get around on its own power, tiring the dog out and helping establish a healthy relationship that lets them know where they are in the hierarchy.

You will always need to be careful of your Chihuahua. There is no weight behind those little frames, so you will not be able to roughhouse with your Chihuahua, ever. You may want to safeguard your home too, especially for young canines that may get overexcited and run around. Training them how to behave will be important, but you can certainly make their home a lot safer for them.

A Warning about Aggression, Barking, and Pampering

One of the biggest problems with Chihuahuas is that they are notoriously obnoxious barkers. Linda Jangula of Chihuahuas Wee Love warns: "One of the most unwanted behaviors is the aggressive barking that some owners deal with on a regular basis. This can be a problem especially when someone rings the doorbell."

They can be downright nasty when strangers come over and the dog has not been properly trained. Baring their teeth and nipping at people is not uncommon for dogs who are overly pampered.

WORDS OF CAUTION
Not Great with Small Children

While it might be tempting to think that small dogs are perfect for small children, the opposite is actually true. Small dogs in general, and Chihuahuas in particular, can be easily injured by children who don't understand how to be gentle. Chihuahuas are also prone to biting. Think twice before bringing a Chihuahua into a home with small children.

You will be responsible for making sure your dog turns out to be a great companion instead of a little dictator in your home. You don't want a dog that feels entitled.

It is going to be very tempting to treat your Chihuahua like a baby – don't give in to that temptation.

Floor Surfaces

Because of their tiny frames, if a Chihuahua gets up speed and goes running around on hard floors, there is going to be no way for your dog to stop before slamming into something. While this is definitely bad for any dog to do, Chihuahuas are not nearly as hardy as larger dogs or even a lot of other small dogs.

Protect your Chihuahua by doing what you should do for any dog – cover the hard floors. Whether you have hardwood floors, vinyl, tile, or something else, put rugs or special mats on these floors to keep your Chihuahua from getting hurt. You could also ban your Chihuahua from going into these areas, especially the garage and kitchen. You don't want to trip over the little guy in the kitchen, so setting down the law and keeping your pup out can be protective of both you and your dog.

Photo Courtesy of Sara Storey

A Wary Breed That Prefers Family

Chihuahuas are not fans of people they don't know. They typically don't feel comfortable around strangers, unless they are constantly exposed to new people during the first year. If you live in an apartment complex, you will want to convince your Chihuahua that the people in the complex are not a threat to keep the barking to a minimum. If you live in a house, you will find that they will be very vocal about any noise they hear outside.

FUN FACT
Celebrity Chihuahua

The most famous Chihuahua in history was Gidget, the dog who starred in the "Yo quiero Taco Bell" commercials in the late 1990s. Gidget also starred in a GEICO commercial and Legally Blonde 2. Gidget passed away in 2009.

Once you let someone into your home, your Chihuahua is going to be giving them wary looks and letting your visitors know that even if you are fine with them being there, the Chihuahua is suspicious of their presence. This can be particularly difficult during renovations and parties. For these times, have a safe space for your Chihuahua to stay so that they are more comfortable and your guests don't feel so wary. The best solution is to properly socialize your Chihuahua so it is not a problem, but this is not always possible. Even a properly socialized Chihuahua may get suspicious with age. Plan how you will handle your Chihuahua when you have visitors to reduce tension.

Ideal Lifestyle

Chihuahuas are small and cute, but they are absolutely not toys, and they do not go well with every lifestyle. Young children are not always a good fit because they may accidentally hurt the dog. However, they are a great dog for older kids, teens, and adults. They are surprisingly great with cats too, though larger dogs may pose a problem for this dog with a Napoleonic complex.

Strengths

Chihuahuas are great alarms. With their large ears and natural wariness, you will have your own little alarm system installed when your puppy becomes an adult, or the day you bring home a dog. They make great travel companions because their size means they are welcome in a lot more places than larger dogs.

They can also be taught to do a lot of interesting tricks if you have the time and patience to teach them. A properly socialized Chihuahua that does tricks is easily one of the best ways to entertain guests and for you to interact with your little companion.

Finally, they are one of the easiest dogs to fulfill exercise requirements. If you have a busy schedule, having two Chihuahuas at home will make for a quick walk after you get through with everything for the day, or as a short break to get out and stretch your legs for a little bit.

Common Exercise Benefits

As mentioned, this is a breed whose exercise needs are incredibly easy to meet. One or two 15-minute walks a day, and that is about all they will need. You won't be able to turn them outside to do their business, so that is one less thing to worry about as well. If it is raining, you can simply play with them for 15 minutes a couple of times, and they will be perfectly content.

You will need to be very careful about feeding them though. It is extremely easy to overfeed a Chihuahua, so make sure that you and everyone in the family stick to the recommend diet and don't let those big eyes fool you into thinking that your dog needs more food.

Beware of Loneliness and Boredom

Chihuahuas are not the kind of dog that enjoys solitude. It is strongly recommended that you have at least one other dog, preferably another Chihuahua, so that your little pup is never left alone. Depending on their personality, being left alone can be either incredibly scary or anger inducing. Neither of these emotions leads to good behavior.

Not Great Learners – Training May Be Rough

Some Chihuahuas are very intelligent, but they also tend to be quite stubborn (a common problem with many intelligent dogs). Those that are not so intelligent, well, they are going to be difficult to train too. There is not a consistent take on the intellect of a Chihuahua, but a lot of breeders will tell you that if you don't take a very firm and consistent approach in the beginning, your dog could be a bit of a problem later.

No matter how smart your canine is, training is going to be something that will take up a good bit of time. You will either need to be very patient or you will need to hire a trainer to help you teach your dog.

A Little Dog Who Loves Family and Other Chihuahuas

They may not be the friendliest dog, but Chihuahuas absolutely love their people. They want to pretty much stay with you all of the time and will be perfectly happy curled up next to you. This makes them great for adults because they are fairly low maintenance (once they are properly trained). They also have incredibly long life spans, which means that when properly socialized and trained, they can stay with you, keeping your lap warm and your hands happily occupied, for up to two decades.

Photo Courtesy of Deborah Butterworth

They also love other Chihuahuas. To make sure your little companion doesn't feel lonely, you really can't go wrong by bringing another Chihuahua into your home. With such a small dog, having several really isn't much different than having one medium- or large-sized dog when it comes to most of your expenses. They will be able to keep each other company, alleviating any fear or unrest they may otherwise feel.

CHAPTER 4.
Finding Your Chihuahua

The process of finding your Chihuahua is both exciting and time consuming. You will need to decide if you want to start with a puppy (and all of the training that entails) or rescue a dog that may have issues but can be trained (typically it requires less time, but a lot more patience). Either way, the Chihuahua you bring home will very likely be with you for a long time, so you can train your canine to be what you want him or her to be.

It is also strongly recommended that you have at least two Chihuahuas. This will make it easier to leave your little guy at home. You don't have to get two puppies at the same time, but you may want to start thinking about getting a second puppy if the training with your first one goes well.

Photo Courtesy of Susan Davies

Adopting from a Breeder

Even though the Chihuahua is a pure breed, and a very small one at that, it is surprisingly healthy. That doesn't mean there aren't some associated genetic health problems with the breed. There are several tests and certifications that are recommended to ensure a Chihuahua is healthy. If the parents do not have these genetic issues, it significantly lowers the likelihood that the puppies will have these problems.

Before you start your search you should know that looking for a good breeder is just the beginning of a lengthy process. According to Barbara Pendergrass of Rafina Chihuahuas: "Be prepared to wait. Chihuahua litters are small, sometimes only one puppy or two." Good breeders aren't going to rush the mother onto the next litter because that is very unhealthy for the mother. There are many Chihuahuas out there, so if you don't want to wait for a puppy you can consider rescuing an adult Chihuahua. Just be aware that you may need to work through some issues that the dog may have.

Once you have decided that you would prefer to wait and work with a puppy, you can get started looking for a great breeder. That should give you plenty of time to prepare for your little pup's arrival.

Finding a Breeder

One of the most important and potentially time-consuming tasks you will have if you decide to start with a puppy is to find a good breeder. Given the Chihuahua's popularity, there are a number of puppy mills and bad breeders that are interested in turning a profit instead of in taking care of the dogs and puppies in their care. You do not want to adopt from a breeder that does not properly care for the dogs. Not only is this unethical, it increases the likelihood that your dog will have serious health problems, and potentially have some behavior problems. Plan to spend several hours over the course of several days looking for the right breeder. Remember, you are going to be in for a wait even if you decide on a breeder in one day, so you may as well take your time and find a breeder you feel you can trust.

Put aside between 30 minutes and an hour to talk with breeders you are considering. The following are some important questions that will help you determine how good the breeder is and where their focus is. If they aren't willing to take the time to talk to you, scratch them off the list. If they say that they are busy and offer another time to talk, make sure to set aside time to call them when they have time. They are taking care of dogs, after all, and that is a time-consuming endeavor.

The following are some questions to ask.

Photo Courtesy of
Emma Prince

Ask each breeder about the required health tests and certifications they have for their puppies. These points are detailed further in the next section, so make sure to check off the available tests and certifications for each breeder. If they don't have all of the tests and certifications, you may want to remove them from consideration. Good breeders not only cover all of these points, they offer a guarantee against the most harmful genetic issues.

Make sure that the breeder always takes care of all of the initial health requirements in the first few weeks through the early months, particularly getting the necessary shots. Puppies require that certain procedures be started before they leave their mother to ensure they are healthy. Vaccinations and worming typically start around six weeks after the puppies are born, and then the procedures need to be continued every three weeks. By the time your puppy is old enough to come home with you, the puppy should be well into the procedures, or even completely through the first phases of these important health care needs.

Ask if the puppy is required to be spayed or neutered before reaching a certain age of maturity. It is possible that you may need to sign a contract that says you will have the procedure done, which you will need to plan for prior to getting your puppy. Typically, these procedures are done in the puppy's best interest.

Find out if the breeder is part of a Chihuahua organization or group. One of the most notable is the Chihuahua Club of America.

Ask about the first phases of your puppy's life, such as how the breeder plans to care for the puppy during those first few months. They should be able to provide a lot of detail, and they should do this without sounding as though they are irritated that you want to know. They will also let you know how much training you can expect to be done prior to the puppy's arrival in your home so you can plan to take over as soon as the puppy arrives. It is possible that the breeder typically starts housetraining (in which case, you are very lucky if you can get on the wait list with them). You will also want to find out if they can provide information on how the puppies have been performing and how quickly they have picked up on the training. You want to be able to pick up from where the breeder left off once your Chihuahua puppy reaches your home.

WORDS OF CAUTION
"Teacup Chihuahuas"

Chihuahuas are already the smallest dog breed, and there is no such thing as a "teacup Chihuahua." Unscrupulous breeders often market the runt of the litter as a "teacup Chihuahua." Assuming the runt isn't born with any significant health problems (runts often are), it will likely grow to be the same size as other Chihuahuas. In fact, Chihuahuas that weigh less than three pounds as adults are prone to a lot more health issues than larger dogs. Don't believe the hype that "teacup Chihuahuas" are somehow smaller than regular Chihuahuas.

See what kind of advice the breeder gives about raising the puppy. They should be more than happy to help guide you to doing what is best for your dog because they will want the puppy to live a happy, healthy life even after leaving the breeder's home. You want a caring breeder that is more interested in the health of the puppies than in the money they make. Yes, you could end up paying a considerable amount of money for your little guy, but you should also get recommendations, advice, and additional care suggestions after the puppy arrives at your home. Breeders that show a lot of interest in the dog's well-being and are willing to answer questions during the dog's entire life span are likely to breed puppies that are healthy.

How many breeds do they manage a year? How many sets of parents do the breeders have? Do they have a regular feeding schedule that the puppies will be accustomed to when they leave their first home? Puppies can take a lot of time and attention, and the mother should have some down time between pregnancies. Learn about the breeder's standard operations to find out if they are taking care of the parents and treating them like valuable family members and not as strictly a way to make money.

Health Tests and Certifications

Chihuahuas are a surprisingly healthy breed when it comes to their genetics. You will definitely need to be very careful with them because they are fragile, but that is tied more to their size than genetics. That does not mean that they are completely in the clear though.

To start with, you need to know what kinds of health problems Chihuahuas tend to have. The following are the recommended health tests to ensure your puppy has the best possible start:

Cardiac Exam

Ophthalmologist Evaluation

Patella Luxation Evaluation

They also have notoriously bad teeth, which you will be able to smell pretty early on. No tests are required for this, but you should ask about the parents' teeth and see what kind of regimen the breeders have to take care of the dogs' teeth. This can help you better tend to your puppy's teeth.

*Photo Courtesy of
Joanna Elliker*

Contracts and Guarantees

Established breeds like the Chihuahua have enough data on them that breeders should feel comfortable guaranteeing the health of their puppies. Even more important, they could (or perhaps should) have some guarantee from you that you will take good care of your puppy, which means signing a contract with the breeder. The contracts and guarantees are protection for the puppies, both showing that they are healthy and to protect you in the event that a puppy is not healthy.

If a breeder has a contract that must be signed, make sure that you read through it completely and are willing to meet all of the requirements prior to signing it. The contracts tend to be fairly easy to understand and comply with, but you should be aware of all of the facts before you agree to anything. Beyond putting down the money for the puppy, signing the contract says that you are serious about how you plan to take care of the puppy to the best of your abilities by meeting the minimum requirements set forth by the breeder. Since the contract focuses on your behavior toward taking care of your dog, it is a good sign that the breeder wants to verify that you are serious about taking care of your puppy. It is probable that the contract will include spaying or neutering the puppy once he or she matures. It may also say that the breeder will retain the registration papers of the puppy, although you can get a copy of them.

The guarantee states what health conditions the breeder guarantees for their puppies. This typically includes details of the dog's health and recommendations on the next steps of the puppy's care once it leaves the breeder's home. Guarantees may also provide schedules to ensure that the health care started by the breeder is continued by the new puppy parent. In the event that a major health concern is found later, the puppy will need to be returned to the breeder. The contract will also explain what is not guaranteed. The guarantee tends to be very long (sometimes longer than the contract), and you should read it thoroughly before you sign it. Guarantees are fairly common with Chihuahuas because of how old the breed is. The guarantees state what the breeder is guaranteeing with your new dog. This usually includes information on the dog's health and recommendations on what the pet owner's next steps should be. For example, it may recommend that you take your puppy to the vet within two days of arriving at your home to ensure that the dog is as healthy as it is believed to be. In the event that a major health concern is found, the puppy will need to be returned to the breeder. It will also explain what is not guaranteed.

In addition to the price for purchasing your dog, Chihuahua contracts ensure certain behavior by the new human parent of a Chihuahua puppy. The contract may also contain naming requirements, health details, and a stipulation for what will happen if you can no longer take care of the canine (the dog usually goes back to the breeder). They also include information on what will happen if you are negligent or abusive.

Puppy Genetics – The Parents

With genetics playing a fairly large role in the personality and health of your puppy, you need to know as much as you can about the parents before the puppy arrives. Good breeders keep detailed histories of their breeding dogs because they understand how important recording this data is. Breeders that are part of official Chihuahua organization are required to keep detailed information, so you know that these breeders are serious about taking good care of their dogs. Review the histories of the parents to find out what to expect from your puppy, especially in terms of personality. Pay close attention to traits, temperament, abilities, clinginess, and any other personality trait you consider to be important.

Of course, this could be an incredibly time-consuming process, but it will help you know about the personality of your puppy. It is well worth all of the time you put into studying and planning because you can help mold your Chihuahua to be an amazing little companion for you and your family.

The more you know about the parents, the better prepared you will be for your puppy. The great breeders will have stories and details about the parents so that you can read about them at your leisure, as well as get a good feel for the breeder.

Selecting Your Puppy

You want to have a visual of your puppy before you bring your new family member home. See if the breeder will provide videos and pictures so that you can check out your puppy after it is born and as it grows during the first few weeks after birth. You also want to get any data on your dog's vet visits and shots.

Selecting a Chihuahua puppy is pretty much the same as selecting any kind of puppy. A lot of it is entirely up to you and what you want in a dog. The experience can be highly entertaining and enjoyable – and ultimately very difficult. As much fun as the process is, you do need to be careful and serious so that you are not swayed by traits that you may find bothersome later.

As you look over the puppies, notice how well each puppy plays with the others. This is a great indicator of just how well your puppy will react to any pets you already have at home.

Photo Courtesy of Elisha Jade Swanson

You also need to look at the puppies as a whole. If you notice that a majority of the puppies exhibit aggressive behavior or seem to tend toward being mistrustful, you may not want to select a puppy from the litter. Similarly, if the puppies appear to be terrified of you, such as keeping their tails tucked or shrinking away from you, that is an indication of the kinds of issues you may encounter with your puppy and training. What you want is a litter that is full of friendly puppies, even if they do not start to greet you immediately. Sometimes they just want to play with their siblings or figure out what is happening before acknowledging you.

Next, notice if there is at least one puppy that is very eager to meet you. Many people take that as a sign that the puppy is the right one for their family. However, that is not always the case. Keep in mind that the puppy or puppies that greet you are more forward and demanding than the ones that sit back and analyze the situation first. The puppies that hang back may be afraid, or, more likely, they just want to understand the situation before they get involved. They are not the alpha types that their eager siblings are. These are the more patient and tame puppies, the ones that may be easier to train.

Pick the puppy that exhibits the personality traits that you want in your dog. If you want a forward, friendly, excitable dog, the first puppy to greet you may be the one you seek. If you want a dog that will think things through and let others get more attention, then this is a mellower dog that may be better for your home.

Pay Attention to the Parents' Personalities

With any breed that has a wide range of potential personalities, you need to see the parents to get an idea of what their personalities are like. This will be a great indication of what your puppy will be like. Not all puppies end up being like their parents (just like with people), but often they exhibit similar personalities. If you have a particular personality you would like for your puppy to have, look for parents that have those personality traits.

You should always meet the parents of the puppies, and a good breeder will always be willing to let you have access to the dogs. They are interested in ensuring that the puppies go to good homes, and showing an interest in the parents shows that you are thinking about the puppy's future.

Linda Jangula of Chihuahuas Wee Love puts it well: "There should be no problem with a legitimate breeder to produce one or both parents on the premises. Ask questions like any noticeable behaviors you might need to be made aware."

Do keep in mind that some Chihuahuas may have had a bad history with humans or may not have been properly trained. If the breeder adopted a dog with a less than happy history, the personality may not reflect the personality your puppy will have with positive experiences. If the dogs have not been well trained, this is also something you can remedy, but you will need to take more time to find out just how the puppies will be managed after birth. You may be starting a bit further behind than with a breeder that takes the time to start potty training puppies. This doesn't mean that there will be a problem with a puppy since you will be getting the little guy more than early enough to train, it just a little extra work for you. Fortunately, with their size, this is not a large problem.

Adopting an Older Dog

An adult Chihuahua may or may not be a much easier starting point for you, depending on how much training the dog has received and what kinds of life experiences the dog has had. Chihuahuas also tend to be less well housebroken because people have the very bad habit of babying them instead of properly training them. This doesn't mean all adult dogs are likely to go to the bathroom all around your home though. Just like training a puppy, it's going to be on you to train your Chihuahua about the expectations that you have.

There will definitely be a warming up period too, so you will want to have a pretty good idea of how the older dog reacts to new situations before bringing the canine home. This will help you prepare for what you need to do, like researching how to fix undesired behavior or to help your new dog feel comfortable in your home.

You can look for rescue Chihuahuas in shelters, rescue sites, and even from breeders. If a person is found in breach of contract from a breeder, the breeder will take the Chihuahua back. The breeder may then choose to sell the puppy or young dog again after some time. In some cases people may not be able to continue to care for their Chihuahua, and may return the canine to the breeder. Breeders will know how to work with returned dogs so there may not be as much work to do with a dog from a breeder (depending on what life was like away from the breeder).

Benefits

Even though there is a higher chance that the dog isn't properly housetrained, you aren't going to be starting from scratch like you would with a puppy. You will still need the same amount of patience though, particularly if you rescue a dog that has had bad experiences with people.

Since Chihuahuas do take time to warm to their people, you can expect that it will take a week or two before your Chihuahua starts to feel comfortable in the new environment. As long as you consistently apply rules and are firm but patient with your new little friend, you won't have to wait nearly so long to start feeling like you have a great companion. Puppies are bouncy and full of energy, but adult Chihuahuas are often calmer and easier to manage. You may prefer to start enjoying time with your dog lounging on the couch instead of having to dedicate a couple of years of training in the basics. Once your dog understands what you want, it is so much easier to have fun together.

Adult Chihuahuas are ideal for older adults with teenagers or no kids. They can also be a great dog for teaching responsibility to older children, as long as the kids understand not to jerk the Chihuahua when he is on the leash. Older Chihuahuas can be great companions for people who can't get out much or who have to stay home for whatever reason. They are content to stay with you and do little to nothing at all, and meeting their exercise needs is incredibly easy.

Rescues

SAD FACTS
Euthanasia in Shelters

Chihuahuas are the second most-euthanized dog breed in shelters, behind only Pit Bulls. Shelters are filled with Chihuahuas that have been dumped by owners who didn't like their feisty personality or thought they would be better with children. Consider adopting or rescuing a Chihuahua rather than buying a puppy. Be warned, however, that a Chihuahua in a shelter may not have had proper socialization or training and may need more attention.

Given the Chihuahua's popularity, there are a lot of rescue organizations for the breed, in addition to their own breeders. Chihuahuas that you get through organizations and breeders have most of the necessary information that is required to sell puppies, meaning you will have the medical history and vaccination information on the dog (although if the human parent was negligent or abusive, the medical history and information may not have been tracked while the dog was with them).

When you contact an organization about adopting an adult Chihuahua, they will require you to apply for the adoption simply because they want to ensure that the dog gets a great home – a place where the dog will be able to live out the rest of his or her days. They will also try to match you up with an adult dog that is ideal for the environment you offer and the lifestyle you live.

Warning about Socialization

Socialization is essential for Chihuahuas. They are incredibly wary of strangers, and this can result in some very aggressive or very anxious behavior. Socialization from an early age will help to make your dog much more comfortable in the world and will make the dog more enjoyable when others are around.

Small dogs are prone to developing small dog syndrome when they are not socialized and trained properly. They can act like little dictators, being aggressive and unpleasant to anyone they are unfamiliar with (and sometimes even with their own people). This makes them generally unpleasant to be around. If not properly socialized at an early age, they can become either very aggressive or very scared of anyone new. Unless you never have people over to visit, this can make it very unpleasant for everyone.

Aggression can go a lot further than just barking too. A Chihuahua that isn't properly socialized may end up nipping, lunging at people, and growling. You don't want them to bare their teeth and bite people, which is why it is essential to teach them that strangers and other dogs aren't as scary or dangerous as your Chihuahua thinks they are. Barking is not always a problem, but the other behaviors are definitely habits you want to avoid or break. By making play dates for your Chihuahua puppy, you will be able to start helping them learn to be happy and excited about meeting other dogs and people instead of feeling a need to intimidate them. Mostly this intimidation reflects your Chihuahua's own anxiety and fear because the canine is not accustomed to being around new people or dogs.

It is also possible that a Chihuahua will be aggressive when you return home after being away. They could feel abandoned or unhappy about your disappearance. This is behavior you will also need to discourage, and is part of the reason adults should always be around during those first few weeks after your dog arrives at your home.

CHAPTER 5.
Preparing for Your Puppy

One of the best things about having a longer wait time for your Chihuahua puppy to arrive is that you will have plenty of time to prepare your home for the arrival of your newest family member. The months while you are waiting should be put to good use preparing your home. While it is always a difficult task to puppy-proof a home (just as difficult as baby-proofing), it is an even more laborious task to prepare for a dog as small as a Chihuahua puppy. It will give you a chance to see your home from your puppy's perspective too.

Two key preparations are your children and other pets. They will need a bit of warning or adjusting prior to the arrival of your little guy. Kids need to be taught to be careful, while other pets will need to get accustomed to changes to your home.

Photo Courtesy of Ramona Kleespies

Preparing Your Kids

Chihuahua puppies are about the same size as a child's toy, so it is understandable if your children try to treat the new pet like a toy. This is why you are going to have to lay down the law and remind your kids about how to properly play with the cute little puppy.

Chihuahuas are not recommended for families with young children, particularly toddlers and kids too young to understand how easy it is to hurt a puppy.

Preparing your older child or teenager is fairly easy because they tend to be far more cognizant of how to properly care for a living creature. Regardless of the age of your kids, make sure there is always an adult present when they play with the Chihuahua. It is going to take a while to learn how to be careful and have fun. Playing with the puppy is going to be exciting, and it will be easy even for teenagers to forget their own strength.

The following are the five golden rules that you should make sure your kids understand fully before the puppy arrives.

1. Always be gentle. Those little Chihuahuas are absolutely adorable, but they are also fairly fragile, despite their sturdy appearance. At no time should anyone play rough with the puppy (or any adult Chihuahua).

   This rule must be applied consistently every time your children play with the puppy. Be firm if you see your children getting too excited or rough. You don't want the puppy to get overly excited either, because puppies may end up nipping or biting. It isn't their fault because they haven't learned better yet – it is the child's fault. Make sure your child understands the possible repercussions if they get too rough.

2. Chase is an outside game. It can be easy for children to forget as they start to play and everyone gets excited. That short game of getting away can quickly devolve into chase, so you will need to make sure your children understand not to start running. Once they get outside, chase is perfectly fine (although you will still need to monitor the play time).

3. Running inside the home is dangerous for two primary reasons. It gives your Chihuahua puppy the impression that your home isn't safe inside because he is being chased, or worse, he gets hurt. Or your puppy will learn that running inside is fine, which can be dangerous as he gets older. One of the last things you want is for your

Prepare
for puppy
Chihuahua
Preparing your kids

Photo Courtesy of
Karen Moore

Chihuahua to go barreling through your home knocking people off their feet because that behavior was fine for him to do that when he was a puppy.

4. Always leave the puppy alone during meal time. This is true whenever your puppy is eating (this can apply to when your kids are eating as well since you don't want your Chihuahua to get accustomed to eating people food while your kids are eating). You don't want your Chihuahua to think that anyone is trying to take the food away from him. Chihuahuas aren't typically aggressive, so it isn't likely he will nip or bite because someone is near his food. However, he can feel inse-

cure about eating if he feels like someone may take his food, which is obviously not fair to your Chihuahua. And older Chihuahuas could be a bit more protective of their food, which could lead to some conflicts. Save yourself, your family, and your Chihuahua trouble by making sure everyone knows that eating time is your Chihuahua's time alone.

5. The Chihuahua should always remain firmly on the ground. This is something that will likely require a good bit of explaining to your children as Chihuahuas look a lot like toys, especially Chihuahua puppies. No one should be picking the puppy up off the ground. You may want to carry your new family member around or play with the pup like he is a baby, but you and your family will need to resist that urge. Kids particularly have trouble understanding since they will see the Chihuahua as being more like a toy than a living creature. The younger your children are, the more difficult it will be for them to understand the difference. It is so tempting to treat the Chihuahua like a baby and to try to carry him like one, but this is incredibly uncomfortable and unhealthy for the canine. Older kids will quickly learn that a puppy nip or bite hurts a lot more than you would think. Those little teeth are incredibly sharp, and you do not want the puppy to be dropped. If your children learn never to pick up the puppy, things will go a lot better. Remember, this also applies to you, so don't make things difficult by doing something you constantly tell your children not to do.

6. All of your valuables should be well out of reach of your children, even your teens. This is about your kids, and not the puppy, being able to reach items. Valuables are not something you want to end up in the puppy's mouth, but that is almost guaranteed to happen if you leave jewelry where someone can easily pick it up. Teenagers are just as likely to grab whatever is within easy reach to play with as the puppy is, so they are nearly as much of a threat to your valuables as tweens and kids who are older than toddlers. If your kids get curious, they are not likely to stop to consider if they should be doing something because they want to know what will happen if they use something while playing with the puppy. The end result will be an incident that will certainly not make you or your children happy when you get upset with them. If you don't want your puppy or children to destroy something valuable, make sure it is never easily accessible.

*Photo Courtesy of
Katie Plant*

Preparing Your Current Dogs

The approach to preparing other dogs is considerably different than preparing a kid for a puppy's arrival. To start with, they aren't going to understand rules. What they do understand are boundaries. They may not understand that there is a puppy coming into the home, but they can definitely understand what it means when you fence off areas of the home. Start with teaching your children, turning your attention to preparing your dogs as your children digest the information (and have it reinforced). Your primary method of preparing your dog or dogs for the arrival of a puppy is to have an area where they know they should not go and to help them understand that you still love them. You should start adjusting your schedule well ahead of the arrival of the puppy, building specific time slots for interacting with your dogs so that they don't start to feel resentful of the puppy.

Here are the things you can do to help ease the transition to having a new Chihuahua around the home.

Think about your dog's personality to help you decide the best way to prepare for that first day, week, and month. Each dog is unique, so you will need to consider your dog's personality to determine how things will go when the new dog arrives. If your dog loves other dogs, this will probably hold true when the puppy shows up. If your dog has any territorial tendencies, you will need to be cautious about the introduction and during the first couple of months so that your current dog learns that the Chihuahua is now a part of the pack. Excitable dogs will need special attention to keep them from getting overly rambunctious when a new dog comes home. You don't want them to be so excited they accidentally hurt the new puppy.

Consider other times when you have had other dogs in your home and how your dog reacted to these other furry visitors. If your canine displayed territorial tendencies, you are going to need to be extra careful with how you introduce your new pup. If you haven't ever invited another dog to your home, schedule a couple of play dates with other dogs at your home before your new Chihuahua arrives. You have to know how your current furry companions will react to a new puppy in the house so you can properly prepare. Meeting a dog at home is very different from encountering one outside the home.

Think about your dog's interactions with other dogs for as long as you have known the dog. Has your dog shown protective or possessive behavior, either with you or others? Food is one of the reasons that most dogs will display some kind of aggression because they don't want anyone trying to eat what is theirs. Some dogs can be protective of people and toys too.

It is important to establish the puppy's area well ahead of the puppy's arrival too. Your dogs need to learn that there is a place in the home where they can't go so that they aren't losing space around the time the puppy comes home. If they are acclimated to the lost space, they may exhibit interest in the puppy, but aren't likely to feel too inclined to go into the area that has been prohibited for some time.

To ensure that your dog doesn't have any reason to want to go into the area, make sure that it doesn't include any of his stuff. All of his toys, furniture, and other items should be in a different space. If he has a favorite seat or couch, the puppy's area should be separate from it – you don't want to take away your dog's favorite spots and resting places, because that will build negative emotions. The puppy should be an addition to the family, and not make the dog feel like he has been replaced.

Make sure your children understand that they are not to throw the older dog's toys and other things into the puppy's area. They also need to understand that the dog cannot go into the area, so they should avoid trying to play with the dog in the space that will be the puppy's living area.

Go ahead and start considering neutral ground where the puppy can meet your other canine or canines. This should not be done in the territory of your dog because he is more likely to feel like the puppy is invading his territory (depending on your dog's personality). Even for mellow dogs, neutral grounds are recommended; somewhere that he won't feel is his place where other dogs shouldn't be. Plan to have at least one other adult present at the time of the initial meeting too.

Photo Courtesy of
Stephanie Lucas
Lucas Chihuahuas

Dangerous Foods

Dogs cannot eat the same foods as humans. Just as a dog can safely eat raw meat that would make a person sick (or kill them), there are foods that humans can eat that can seriously hurt a dog. Chihuahuas are particularly at risk because of their size. It will not take much of these dangerous foods to kill a Chihuahua.

You are probably aware that your dogs should not eat chocolate, but there are many other foods that will give a dog's digestive track trouble and foods that are toxic to a dog. These foods should never be given to a dog of any size, but even small quantities of any one of these items could be lethal to a Chihuahua.

The following are foods that are on the Do Not Eat list for dogs.

- Apple seeds
- Chocolate
- Coffee
- Cooked bones (they can kill a dog when the bones splinter in the dog's mouth or stomach)
- Corn on the cob (it is the cob that is deadly to dogs; corn off the cob is fine, but you need to make sure that your Chihuahua cannot reach any corn that is still on the cob)
- Grapes/raisins
- Macadamia nuts
- Onions and chives
- Peaches, persimmons, and plums
- Tobacco (your Chihuahua will not know that it is not a food and may eat it if it is left out)
- Xylitol (a sugar substitute in candies, baked goods, and some peanut butters)
- Yeast

In addition to these potentially deadly foods, there is a long list of other things that your dog shouldn't eat for health reasons. The Canine Journal has a lengthy list of foods that should be avoided. It includes foods like alcohol and other substances that people give dogs, thinking that it is funny. Remember that dogs have a very different metabolism and the effect that these foods have on them is much stronger than the effect they have on people.

For the sake of your Chihuahua's health, it is best just to keep all of these foods out of reach, even if the items are non-lethal.

Hazards to Fix

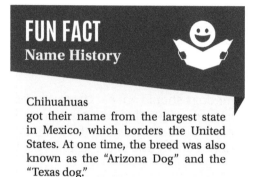

FUN FACT
Name History

Chihuahuas got their name from the largest state in Mexico, which borders the United States. At one time, the breed was also known as the "Arizona Dog" and the "Texas dog."

Preparing your home for a puppy is as time consuming as it is for a baby. Plan to spend at least a few months (if not more) to get your home ready. It wouldn't be a bad idea to start preparing your home around the time you start looking for a breeder because there are going to be a lot of things to do for the arrival of such a small dog. The extra effort you put into preparing your home will be well worth it, as you will give your little Chihuahua a safe place, teaching him that the big world isn't something to fear.

This section details the areas of the home where you should really focus your attention to make sure you don't miss anything important that could be dangerous for your little darling.

Also, be aware that all puppies, including Chihuahuas, will try to eat virtually anything, even if it isn't food. Nothing is safe – not even your furniture. Puppies will gnaw on wood and metal. Anything within their reach is fair game. Keep this in mind as you go about puppy-proofing your home.

Kitchen and Eating Areas

Easily the most dangerous room in the house, the kitchen is a combination of poisonous foods, dangerous items, and poisons. It is the room where you should probably plan to spend most of your time when puppy-proofing your home. Everything you would do to protect a small child in this room is something you will need to do for a Chihuahua. This could include making sure the cabinets are locked in case your Chihuahua is clever enough to figure out how to open them. He is going to be following you around like a little shadow once he is allowed out of his puppy area, and he will be learning that things open. Some of them are clever enough to be able to get into cabinets, especially the cabinets where you do not want them to go.

You will need to make sure that all poisons are put in places where your Chihuahua cannot reach them (whether in the kitchen, in other rooms of the house, the garage, and all outdoor areas). Chihuahuas can get into nearly everything, and your little friend will be exploring a lot when given the opportunity. Anything that may catch your attention or draw your interest is worth a try – that's what centuries have taught them. Being vigilant about making sure he can't hurt himself is vital to keeping your Chihuahua safe. At no time should you leave poisons in an unsecured place.

Trash cans are equally dangerous because that's where all kinds of great smells exist to lure your Chihuahua to misbehave. Having just gone over the list of foods that they shouldn't eat, leaving any of these foods in the trash is a serious risk to a Chihuahua puppy. There are also things like poisons, plastics, and other items your puppy may think should be taste tested. Just because your Chihuahua is small does not mean that it is impossible for him to knock over a trash can. Take all of the necessary precautions, such as getting a trash can you can lock or storing it under a cabinet that is locked. This will keep your puppy from getting into too much trouble or creating a mess for you to clean up.

All electrical cords need to be up and out of reach of little Chihuahua puppies that could be curious as to what cords are and how they work. You don't want the puppy to trip or get tangled in a cord any more than you want your puppy to try to eat the cord. Then there are things like blender cords and other wires that connect to heavier items that you don't want pulled onto your puppy. Cords aren't just electrical either – if you have long cords for your blinds, these need to be shortened or put where they will not fall to the floor where your Chihuahua can reach them.

Bathroom and Laundry

The dangers in the bathroom are almost the same as for those in the kitchen, just in a smaller space. There are so many poisons in bathrooms that keeping the doors closed could be the best way to go. Since that is really not an option for many families (particularly if you have children or teenagers who are likely to forget), you need to make sure to keep everything that could attract attention and danger locked up or out of reach.

Do keep the toilet seat closed, and don't use any automatic cleaners. Some Chihuahuas have been clever enough to learn how to drink out of toilets, which means it is up to you to keep the toilets inaccessible to your curious pup. If the toilet seat is left open (as is bound to happen occasionally), make sure there aren't any poisons in it by avoiding having any automatic cleaners in the water.

Though it doesn't at first seem likely, the laundry room can actually be a dangerous room as well. The easiest way to deal with it is to keep the door shut if you can. Many families keep a number of miscel-laneous items (including poisons) in the laundry room because it is kind of a catch-all place. You may only have bleach, laundry detergent, dryer sheets, and other clothing cleaners, but even those can be very danger-ous to a Chihuahua. This is particularly true of items like laundry pods. You also need to keep all dirty clothing off of the floor – if for no other reason than to keep your Chihuahua puppy from dragging the most em-barrassing garments all around your home. There is also a chance that your Chihuahua may try to eat some of the clothing, which would not be great for your Chihuahua. Nor is it a great time for you if you have to take an emergency trip to the vet's office or animal hospital.

Other Rooms

Most of the other rooms of the house should be relatively safe since people don't tend to keep chemicals outside of cabinets.

You will need to do a thorough inspection for cords that are low to the ground or within jumping distance of your Chihuahua's reach. All of these will need to be secured well above where your Chihuahua can reach. Don't forget about spaces like the computer area and entertain-ment center where there is typically a lot of wiring. You will also need to check the window cords to make sure they are too high for your puppy to reach.

All cleaning products need to be stored some place that your puppy cannot go, too. If you keep objects like air fresheners on surfaces, make sure that these areas are not places where your Chihuahua can go. Since most Chihuahuas are allowed on couches and beds, you will need to clear off end tables and nightstands – and anything that contains chem-icals and is accessible from the furniture.

If you have a fireplace, all cleaning supplies and tools will need to be stored in a place where the puppy cannot get into them. The area where the fire is also needs to be made inaccessible to curious puppies. This needs to be true all of the time so that your puppy does not play in the ashes or with the wiring in the fireplace.

If you have stairs in your home, they will need to be cordoned off so that your puppy cannot try to go up or down them. Tables (including end tables and coffee tables) need to be cleared of dangerous objects, such as scissors, sewing equipment, pens, and pencils. All valuables should be kept in safe locations away from furniture where your puppy will go.

If you have a cat, you are going to need to keep the litter box up off of the floor. It needs to be somewhere that your cat can easily get to but your Chihuahua cannot. Since this could include teaching your cat to use the new area, it is something you should do well in advance of the puppy's arrival. You don't want your cat to be undergoing too many significant changes all at once. The puppy will be enough of a disruption – if your cat associates the litter box change with the puppy, you may find your cat protesting the change by refusing to use the litter box.

Garage

The best way to deal with the garage is to make sure your Chihuahua cannot go into it. There are so many dangerous things in garages that keeping all puppies out is the best policy. However, given their size, it is certain that the little Chihuahua will manage to slip into the garage when you don't expect it. With all of the chemicals, sharp implements, and other dangerous tools that are stored there, the garage is one of the most hazardous places in any home. Never leave your Chihuahua alone in the garage, even when it is an adult. It is likely that your puppy will be in the garage when you take car trips, which is why it is important to puppy-proof it.

All items related to your car and its maintenance have to be stowed high off the ground where your puppy cannot go, and a locked area is the safest way to store it. This includes all lubricants, oils, and cleaners, as well as wrenches and tools. You will need to do the same for all of your lawn maintenance items, bike tools, and anything used for heavy machinery or that includes chemicals.

Puppies will chew anything, including tires, cans, tools, and bags. Everything that can be placed up high or locked in a cabinet should be.

You will need to do this with all of your hobbies too. Things like fishing tackle are incredibly dangerous and should be stored somewhere out of reach, too. You will need to make sure there is nothing hanging over the countertops where the puppy can try to pull it down.

The best way to deal with the problem is to enter the garage from a toddler's perspective. Anything that you would immediately move for a toddler should be moved for your puppy. Get down low and see the garage from your puppy's perspective. If you keep your cars in the garage, you can move them out to get a better view. Move anything that could be a potential danger.

Outdoors and Fencing

While you should definitely make the backyard safe, you should never send your Chihuahua out alone. You will always need to stay very close to your dog to protect him.

53

Some breeders suggest adding another layer of protection for your dog. Since birds can be remarkably fast, you can purchase netting for an area of your yard where your Chihuahua will do activities like go to the bathroom. Since this breed is the same size as a cat (and puppies are even smaller than that), you should not have your Chihuahua puppy outside without a leash. If you want your Chihuahua to learn to use the bathroom outside, have a small fenced in area with a net over it that predators cannot get through. All it takes is for you to turn your back for a moment, and a bird of prey can take off with your Chihuahua. Netting will make it difficult for birds and other predators (including other dogs, large cats, and raccoons) to enter the area and take off with your Chihuahua.

Go over your yard the same way you did the garage, making sure there are no chemicals or dangerous items that can hurt your puppy. If your puppy manages to get out of the safe area, the items in your yard are as hazardous as any predators, and are a much more constant danger. Make sure chemicals, tools, and other items are stored where your puppy cannot get to them. Any hanging material on outside tables or items should be removed or shortened. Check that there aren't any gaps or problems with the fencing that your puppy could wiggle through if he gets out of the safe area. You also need to make sure there aren't any potentially dangerous plants that your puppy might munch on. There is a lot to do outside, but typically less than you have to do inside. Remember, you should always be outside with your Chihuahua keeping an eye on the puppy or adult, even in secure areas, because he is more than capable of escaping through the smallest holes and gaps. A watchful eye will keep him safe, and it is much easier than dealing with the curiosity of a cat. The Chihuahua will be happy to romp outside for a bit, but will be just as content to go out, go to the restroom, and get back inside.

Supplies and Tools to Purchase and Prepare

Planning for your puppy's arrival means buying a lot of supplies up front. You will need a wide range of items. If you start making purchases around the time you identify the breeder, you can stretch out your expenses over a longer period of time. This will make it seem a lot less expensive than it actually is, though it is much cheaper than what is needed for most other breeds. The following are recommended items:

- Playpen (optional)
- Crate
- Bed
- Leash
- Doggy bags for walks
- Collar

- Tags
- Puppy food
- Water and food bowls (sharing a water bowl is usually okay, but your puppy needs his or her own food dish if you have multiple dogs)
- Toothbrush (very important for this breed, and you may want to buy a couple)
- Brush
- Toys

For training treats, you actually have it very easy. Instead of buying the more expensive treats, Cheerios are just as effective and much cheaper. One little piece of cereal for listening is all it takes, and your Chihuahua is not likely to get tired of eating them since this is not a breed that is particularly picky about food.

If there is anything else you want, feel free to add it to the list.

Health care items like flea treatments can be purchased, but they are expensive and you won't need them for a while. Puppies should not be treated until they reach a specified age.

Planning the First Year's Budget

The costs for having a puppy is a lot more than you would think, but it's still less expensive to bring in a puppy than a new infant. You will need to have a budget, which is another reason to start purchasing supplies a few months in advance. When you buy the items you need, you will begin to see exactly how much you will spend a month. Of course there are some items that are one-time purchases, such as the crate, but many other items you will need to purchase regularly, like food and treats.

You also need to have a budget for the one-time purchases too. This means doing some research ahead of time for those purchases. It is almost guaranteed that you are going to overspend, but you will want to stick to the budget as much as possible.

Begin budgeting the day you decide to get your puppy. Be sure to include the adoption cost, which is typically higher for a purebred dog than for a rescue. If you want to rescue a Chihuahua, decide where you want to find your newest family member. Plan to spend a lot of time researching costs for bringing your puppy or adult dog home, as well as the other costs.

The vet and other healthcare costs should be included in your budget. Regular vaccinations are required, and an annual checkup should be included in the budget. Vet prices vary a lot between different states, even between cities, making it difficult to average the cost. It is always worth the cost, but you will want to know what it will be before your puppy arrives.

If you want to join a Chihuahua organization, budget for the activities. There are a lot of things you can do with Chihuahuas if you want to be with other puppy parents. Fortunately, this is not necessary because Chihuahuas love to lounge at home and don't require much time outside of the home to be perfectly content.

Keep Things Out of Reach

This is fairly easy as your Chihuahua is too small to reach much of anything. Keep in mind that your dog can still jump, so you will need to learn to keep items that your canine might want to chew in locations where your dog cannot reach them, even if they jump up. If you have tablecloths, your Chihuahua could pull them, so you will want to use shorter cloths so that your Chihuahua cannot reach them. This is safer both for your dog and the stuff you keep on your tables. Don't forget that this is true for any table. Linda Jangula of Chihuahuas Wee Love warns about the trouble your Chihuahua could potentially get into: "Drapes, tablecloths, anything hanging within their reach makes for lots of fun, so beware of their smart, cunning abilities." Pulling these things down is not only messy, but potentially dangerous as any heavy or metal objects can seriously injure or kill your puppy.

The Puppy Area

Chihuahuas are a bit different than other dogs because they require so little space to be comfortable. While most puppies will need to have a fenced off area, Chihuahuas can get by in a space the size of – or in an actual – playpen. As Jeanne Eubanks of Uey's Chihuahuas puts it, "A fenced in playpen with everything they need in the playpen is perfect."

By getting a playpen for your pup, you will be minimizing on encroaching on space for other pets while making it difficult for the puppy to get out. You can also fence off a small area for your puppy, an area roughly the size of a playpen, but make sure that children and dogs understand long before the puppy arrives that they cannot knock the fencing down.

You can also get gates and block off a small area for your puppy. Do make sure that it is sturdy enough to withstand children or other dogs knocking it over. Give it a test from both sides. Just because Chihuahuas are not big does not mean they cannot knock gates down if they set their mind to it. Since they are small, you need to make sure that the gaps are much smaller so that they cannot squeeze their heads through only to be stuck. One of the last things you want is a Chihuahua puppy stuck in the fence or running around with a gate attached to it.

Chihuahuas are going to be right there with you wherever you go, but their size means that they aren't able to reach many areas. It is very important to keep a lot of things out of their reach, especially food and items that they can reach from the couch or bed. They can knock things over, like plants and decorations when you are away and that can be very dangerous. Chihuahuas can have anxiety issues, and they may knock things over while trying to look out of windows in an effort to see you. You will need to spend time puppy proofing your home so that your little guy does not get hurt or chew on things of value or that are special to you. You won't be able to do anything about table and chair legs until your Chihuahua has learned not to chew on furniture, so keep the little fellow in a penned in area. This will be safer for your dog and your furniture.

CHAPTER 6.
The First Week

The moment your little Chihuahua comes through that door, everything is going to change. Years from that day, you are going to look back and remember a lot of details and all of the excitement. Every puppy is a bundle of possibilities that requires a lifetime commitment by you to help the puppy reach his full potential. With a breed as long-lived as the Chihuahua, you want him to get the best possible start to have a full, healthy, happy life.

The first week is critical to the development of your puppy as that is when you establish the dynamic in the home and make the puppy begin to feel safe in a new environment. These are the early days of seeing your Chihuahua reach his or her full potential. With all of the puppy-proofing already done, you now have the daunting task of assisting your little guy in learning how to play, where to go to the bathroom, and finding out that his new home is a great place to live.

Preparation and Planning

Just like you have to prepare your home and yard, you still have some final tasks to do before your new puppy enters the home. You should start with completing a final check of your home to verify your work. From the puppy's area to food and toys, you should have everything set and ready for your new arrival. Anything that you can do before the Chihuahua's arrival will help you to better enjoy your time together when he gets there so that you don't have to try to do stuff on the fly –

you are going to have to do that enough without leaving too many things to do for later.

During the final week before the puppy arrives, create a list of everything that your puppy needs for the first day. The following should help you get started:

- Food
- Bed
- Crate
- Toys

- Water and food dishes
- Leash
- Collar
- Treats

Verify that you have everything on the list out and ready for use before your Chihuahua walks through the door. You don't want to have to run out and buy them after the puppy is home, partly because you will want those things readily available, and partly because you don't want to miss time with your newest family member as you start to establish a routine.

If you plan to have a fence to keep the puppy penned up in a specific area of the home, have the gates set up and verify that they cannot be knocked over or circumvented. Your Chihuahua probably can't knock the gates over, but your puppy is very likely small enough to slip through most gaps.

Set up a schedule for the puppy's care. Know that the plans are going to change, but you need to have a starting point. This will ensure that people complete their assigned tasks and help to make your puppy feel safe – dogs prefer structure, so schedules are a great source of security for them. Tweak the schedule as it becomes clear that changes are needed, but try to keep it as close to the original schedule as possible. Having a schedule in place before the puppy arrives will make it a lot easier than if you try to establish the routine after his arrival. The Chihuahua is going to have more than enough energy to keep you busy, making it difficult to make a plan after his arrival.

The schedule should include a bathroom break after every meal. There is a good chance your puppy will need to go then, and this will help to establish where the right places are to use the bathroom. Since they should be trained to go inside, you definitely want them to start learning where it is an acceptable place to go as early as possible. If the trainer has already started the housetraining, you don't want to lose the progress your puppy has made.

Have a final meeting with all of the family members to make sure all of the rules are remembered and understood before the puppy arrives

Photo Courtesy of
Jackie Beffa

and is a distraction. Children will need special training in how to handle the puppy, and you are going to need to be very strict in making sure they aren't too rough with the pup. Verify that your children understand that they are not allowed to play with the puppy unless there is an adult supervising them. Determine who is going to be responsible for primary puppy care, including who will be the primary trainer. To help teach younger children about responsibility, a parent can pair with a child to manage the puppy's care. The child will be responsible for activities like keeping the water bowl filled and feeding the puppy, and a parent can oversee the performance of the tasks.

Do one more inspection from the ground level in every room of the house and the garage. This should be done a few hours before the puppy arrives to make sure that all of the risks have been removed (habits can be difficult to break, so make sure everything is in order).

The Ride Home

Chihuahua training happens from the moment your puppy is given into your care. The rules and hierarchy should start to be established from that first car ride home.

As tempting as it is to cuddle and try to make your Chihuahua feel comfortable, you will need to put the Chihuahua in a crate for the ride – you cannot start by making an exception. Your puppy is learning from the very beginning. Anything that he can do to make you drop your guard and let him get away with stuff, he is going to use later, and he can be incredibly stubborn about doing things his way if you are lenient in the beginning. As difficult as it will be, you will need to be firm and consistent with your Chihuahua puppy.

Two adults should be present on the first trip. Ask the breeder if the puppy has been in a car before, and, if not, the second adult can act as comforter. The puppy will be in the crate, but the adult can provide soothing words and pets to let the little pup know that everything will be all right. It will definitely be scary because the puppy no longer has mom, siblings, or known people around, so having someone present to talk to the puppy will make it a little less of an ordeal for the little guy.

This is the time to start teaching your puppy that car trips are enjoyable. This means making sure that the crate is securely in place instead of being loose to move around during the drive. You really don't want to terrify the puppy by letting the crate slide around while the puppy is inside it, sitting helplessly. That will only teach your Chihuahua that cars are as terrifying as they look.

Go straight home – do not take your new puppy anywhere else. Apart from visiting the vet and taking walks close to home, don't plan to take your puppy anywhere for the first couple of weeks. Linda Jangula of Chihuahuas Wee Love warns, "When a very young Chihuahua goes home, the first thing people have a tendency to do is take the puppy to visit friends or take it shopping." This is a terrible idea for every breed, but particularly for Chihuahuas. A Chihuahua can go into a hypoglycemic shock if he gets too tired or hungry. Nor does he need to learn to fear the world. Socialization comes later. The first week is about letting him get used to you and your home.

First Night Frights

Photo Courtesy of Tasha Snitch

Your puppy's first night will almost certainly be a terrifying experience for him. Away from mommy and any siblings, as well as the humans the puppy has come to know at his old home, fear is a reasonable response. As understandable as this may be, there is only so much comfort you can give without going overboard. Just like with a baby, the more you respond to cries and whimpering, the more you are teaching a puppy that negative behaviors result in desired results. Prepare for a very difficult balancing act to provide reassurance that things will be all right without coddling your puppy.

You should have a sleeping area established for the puppy prior to his arrival. It should include a bed, and probably a crate or pen. Your bed is not an acceptable place for the puppy to sleep. The entire puppy area should be blocked off so that no one can get into it (and the puppy cannot get out) during the night. It should also be close to where people sleep so that the puppy does not feel abandoned.

To make things a little more familiar, you could also request that something that smells like the mother be provided. The best way to get an item that smells familiar to the little guy is for you to send a blanket along that the breeder can place with the mother for a few days before the puppy comes home. The blanket can then also travel with the puppy in the car on the way to your place.

Things like sounds may attract your puppy's attention, and those unfamiliar sounds can be scary. Minimizing noises can help make the first night a little less terrifying. You have grown accustomed to all kinds of background noises, but many of them will probably be new to your puppy.

Your puppy is certainly going to make noises over the course of the night, and you cannot think of them as an inconvenience, regardless of if they keep you from sleeping. The puppy is sad and scared, so endure it – the puppy has it much harder than you do. Do not move the puppy away from you, even if the whimpering keeps you awake. Being moved away from people will only scare the puppy more, reinforcing the anxiety and fear of your home. Doing this on the first night will make the wrong impression, giving your puppy a terrible feeling about what life will be like with you. Over time, simply being close to you at night will be enough to reassure your puppy that everything will be all right.

Not getting much sleep should be something you expect during that first week or so (just like with an infant). That's why you should plan for the first night to be over a weekend, holiday, or night when sleep is not as essential. The puppy's second day in your home should be about the puppy, not about returning to your normal schedule. Make sure you don't have work or anything pressing to do the next day so that the lack of sleep isn't too disruptive. Losing sleep is part of the deal of bringing a puppy into your home. Fortunately, it doesn't take as long to get a puppy acclimated as it takes with a human infant, so your normal schedule can resume more quickly.

One of the hardest things to do is to ignore the whimpering. You will learn to distinguish what the different sounds your puppy makes mean, but in the beginning, you need to use your best judgment. That first night, the whimpering is fear of the situation and longing for home. Reassure the puppy once or twice, but just let the puppy be to cry it out the rest of the time.

If you give in, over time the whimpering, whining, and crying will get louder. Spare yourself the trouble later by teaching the puppy that it won't work.

Do not let your puppy into your bed that first night – or any other night – until they are fully housetrained. Once a Chihuahua learns that the bed is accessible, you cannot train him not to hop up on it. If he is not housetrained, you are going to need a new bed because everywhere is a place to use the bathroom in those early days.

The last thing that is going to cut into your sleep is the need for regular bathroom breaks. Set up something in the puppy's space, but make sure that the puppy uses it over the course of the night. You aren't going to be staggering outside with your little puppy because of all of the night predators, so you have it easier than most new puppy owners. That does not mean you can get lazy though. You need to keep to a schedule, even during the night, to train your puppy where to use the bathroom. Puppies will need to go to the bathroom every two to three hours, and you will need to get up several times during the night to make sure he understands that he is to always go to the bathroom on the wee pad. If you don't enforce the rule the first night, you are going to have a difficult time training him that he cannot go in the house later.

First Vet Visit

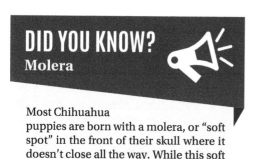

DID YOU KNOW?
Molera

Most Chihuahua puppies are born with a molera, or "soft spot" in the front of their skull where it doesn't close all the way. While this soft spot will close in most puppies as they grow, some Chihuahuas keep this feature throughout their lives.

This is going to be a difficult task because you may feel a bit like you are betraying your puppy (especially with those big eyes begging you to make it stop). However, it is necessary to do this within the first day or two of your puppy's arrival. You need to establish a baseline for the puppy's health so that the vet can track progress and monitor the puppy to ensure everything is going well as the puppy develops and ages. Chihuahuas that have giardia are likely to develop hypoglycemia. You need to have your Chihuahua checked to make sure the little dear is healthy.

It also creates a rapport between the Chihuahua and the vet, which can help later on too. The initial assessment gives you more information about your puppy, as well as giving you a chance to ask the vet questions and get advice.

It is certain to be an emotional trip for both of you, but in the beginning your puppy may be excited. With so much to sniff and so many other pets to meet, there will be a lot for your Chihuahua to take in. Both people and other pets are likely to attract your puppy's attention. This is a chance for you to work on socializing the puppy, although you will need to be careful. Always ask the owner if it is all right for your puppy to meet any other pet, and wait for approval before letting your puppy say hello. Pets at the vet's office are very likely to not be feeling great, which means they may not be very affable. You don't want a grumpy older dog or a sick animal to nip, hurt, or scare your puppy. Nor do you want your puppy to be exposed to anything potentially dangerous while still going through the shots. You want the other animal to be happy about the meeting (though not too excited) so that it is a positive experience for your puppy.

Having a positive first experience with other animals can make the visit to see the vet less terrifying, and even a little fun. This can help your puppy feel more at ease during the visits to see the vet.

The Start of Training

Your Chihuahua's training begins the moment your puppy enters your car or your home, and it really doesn't ever stop. The first few weeks will have some more intense training as you are teaching the basics, and this will serve as the foundation for all other training that you may want to do.

The focus during these first few weeks is to minimize undesirable behavior.

Barking

Chihuahuas are known for being vocal. If you want your puppy to be quieter, you must start during the first week. It will probably mean a few extra treats over the next few months (this is when Cheerios are fantastic), but that is how you will teach your puppy what "quiet" means. However, you may want to avoid giving your puppy treats during the first week. There are good odds that his tummy will be a little upset, so don't compound that by giving him extra food. Your puppy will also be noisy when trying to get your attention, so you will be training yourself to react in a certain way to the noises as well.

The Leash

Leash training will probably be pretty easy since your Chihuahua will want to check out the area around your home. The training is actually just as much for you as for the puppy. Never jerk your puppy on the leash. In the beginning, don't let your children walk the puppy unless they are old enough and responsible enough not to pull hard. It is very easy to hurt a Chihuahua's neck, and that can cause other problems. You will need to start finding ways to keep your puppy walking without being forceful.

Given how easy it is to hurt their necks, consider leash training with harnesses. Your pup probably has not used one before, so there may be a learning period when he has to get accustomed to using a harness instead of being able to move around freely like he does at home (his boundaries are marked by walls, doors, and gates, not by something on his little body). Never drag your puppy. If your Chihuahua does not care for walks, playing inside can give him ample exercise as long as you make sure to do it several times a day for 15 to 30 minutes at a time. To help your puppy get accustomed to being on a leash, you can let the little puppy explore parts of your house while being supervised and wearing the leash. You will need to keep an eye on your puppy the entire time that you let him drag the leash around so that he doesn't get hurt or choked.

Teaching Respect

Respect is a part of training, especially for a dog like the Chihuahua. Whatever behavior you teach now will be lessons that your puppy carries forward. You want to teach your puppy to respect you without fearing you. Consistency is the best way to do that. Do not make exceptions during the first week because you will be fighting that lesson essentially for the rest of your dog's life.

Training to Not Shred

Some Chihuahuas will shred anything you leave in their space. Watch for this kind of behavior when he is young and be prepared to stop him right in his little tracks.

This will be one of the quickest ways to discourage shredding. You may not want to start in the first week or two, but your puppy probably won't try to shred things just yet. Do be watchful for it though, and as soon as your Chihuahua starts to tear something up, intervene.

Grooming – Constant Shedders

Most breeders say that Chihuahuas don't shed much. The worst of it happens when the seasons change. However, they do still shed.

Fortunately, they are very small, making it incredibly easy to brush them every day. It is the perfect way to bond with your little guy in the beginning too. He will enjoy the attention and affection, and you will be happy to have a fewer dog hairs in your food. It can also help to relieve stress at the end of a rough day. Petting dogs has proven to be a significant stress reliever, so there is a lot to get from this daily interaction.

Be aware that short-haired Chihuahuas actually shed more than the long-haired variety. It is unexpected but true. Since it isn't time consuming with either type of Chihuahua, daily brushings still won't take a long time and can be very enjoyable.

Plan to Stay Home and Be Low Key

Chihuahuas that are properly socialized and trained can be among some of the lowest maintenance dogs because they don't require going outside. During inclement weather, they can get adequate exercise just from being home playing with you.

The key is that they have to be properly trained and socialized. This can be a lot of work up front, but it is worth it in the end for such a fantastic, easy to manage dog. They will be a great travel companion or a fantastic lounge buddy – whatever the situation calls for.

CHAPTER 7.
The First Month

After all of the excitement and activity of the first week, you will probably start to settle into a routine. You will have an idea of what your puppy is like, and a relationship will already be established. You may also be quite tired, but you will be able to see some progress – it will be a happy kind of tired.

Having a basic understanding of your puppy's personality means you will be able to see what motivates your puppy best (praise is easily the best way to get a Chihuahua to act, but food is a very close second). This will make the first month a bit easier than the first week, and by the end of that month, you will have a much better idea of how to progress with training and playtime.

Photo Courtesy of Emma Prince

At this stage, your Chihuahua will seem adorable and cute, which may make you drop your guard a bit. Fight that urge. You must continue to be firm and consistent in your approach so that the training sticks. Some Chihuahuas learn quickly while others are fairly slow learners, but none of them will do what you want them to do if you aren't firm and consistent. Training should also be done daily, if only for short periods of time, to get your puppy used to the idea of training. You should see some results of the training by the end of the month, although the results may not seem very big. Most puppies start slow. Training is going to take a while, but in the end, you will have a great companion that travels well and keeps you company at home.

Not Up to Full Strength

You will probably be quite excited about playing with your puppy, but you need to be careful of a few things.

Photo Courtesy of Kristina Lesoine

1. When they get tired and hungry they can become hypoglycemic. This means that they have low blood sugar, which can be fatal. Feeding them will fix the problem, but it is best to not have the puppy exercising for long periods of time.

2. Their necks can be easily hurt when a human jerks on the leash. Given their tiny size, they are not going to be able to keep up with you very well. It is easier to be patient when you stay close to home, and reduces the chance that you will pick up the puppy to move faster.

3. They may fit in a bag, but they aren't potty trained yet. Any bag you use is almost certainly going to be ruined.

Even as an adult, your Chihuahua isn't going to be up for long hikes or walks, but as a puppy outdoor exercise is going to be pretty much a quick jaunt outside before heading home. Daily exercise will need to be tailored to your puppy's abilities, and staying home will make it easier to be safe. For example, you can walk your puppy around the yard on a leash. Since you should never let your puppy be outside on its own, this can be a great way to train your puppy without worrying about animals of prey.

Walks will need to be kept short and exercise should be limited to short periods of time, though you can have several exercise sessions over the course of the day. Typically, the exercise sessions will end with a nice puppy nap, meaning you won't be overly tired but will have time to do the things you need to do without feeling like your puppy misses you. The puppy will still need to sleep in the designated puppy area because when that little pup wakes, you may not be in the room.

By the time the first month wraps up, your puppy will have a bit more stamina. Over the course of the month, and subsequent months, you will need to adjust your schedule to accommodate longer walks and play sessions. Longer exercise sessions mean fewer sessions, which can actually free up more time in your schedule. Just make sure to monitor your Chihuahua's energy levels.

Setting the Rules and Sticking to Them

Chihuahuas love to be with their people. Since they are so cute and can be so affable, you are much more likely to give in to the urge to not train your dog today, thinking that you can train him later. This is something that your Chihuahua is going to notice, and he will try to use that to get his way. Although you may feel that your puppy is too young for a firm approach, it isn't. Puppies need a firm approach, perhaps even more so as you are establishing a baseline. Exceptions to the rules should never be made in the early days if you want the training to stick.

By failing to keep your training consistent, you are establishing a bad dynamic for yourself and your Chihuahua since it will be difficult to convince your dog that you are serious later. Inadvertently, you have already taught your puppy that listening to you is optional. With the right look or action, the Chihuahua can get you to lose focus.

Training is important to keep him from hurting himself or destroying your items. It will keep him from being difficult to manage later. You do not want a little Napoleon trying to dictate things around your home.

A firm consistent approach with your Chihuahua is best for both of you. You want to have fun together, but that also means making sure your Chihuahua knows that there are some things that are required, including listening to you.

Early Socialization – Essential for a Happy Chihuahua

Chihuahuas are tiny – most things in the world are larger than they are, including most house cats. Some members of the breed tend to be either overly aggressive to compensate for their size, or they are fearful of everything. Neither of these traits is healthy for your Chihuahua. To make the world an easier place to feel comfortable, you need to ensure that socialization is something you actively work to do with your puppy.

Regular walks where he can meet people are perfect. It teaches your puppy to be comfortable with others instead of feeling a need to constantly bark at strangers. They don't need much exercise. Jeanne Eubanks of Uey's Chihuahuas says "a 15 minute walk once or twice a day is perfect for them, especially if they can socialize with humans during the walk."

Squeezing socialization into the exercise schedule is the best way to take care of two things at the same time.

Treats and Rewards vs. Punishments

Training and treats are so closely thought of together that it can be difficult to consider anything else as an effective means of training your dog. Second to treats, people think of punishment as a way of dissuading dogs from undesirable behavior. Although these have been the typical methods used in training, there are seri-

FUN FACT
Wedding Bouquet Chihuahuas

In Mexico in the late 1800s and early 1900s, grooms often gave their brides bouquets of flowers with Chihuahuas inside.

ous problems with both, particularly with Chihuahuas. Teaching a puppy proper behavior is a balancing act to make sure that you are firm, but not cruel, so you should provide rewards, but use something better than food.

Positive reinforcement can be an effective way to train Chihuahuas. Food is an obvious choice, but you have to be very careful not to overfeed your puppy. You don't want the little pup to get accustomed to eating too much, especially as they become adults and no longer have a rapid metabolism. Starting with treats is best, but you should quickly begin using praise and extra petting as the primary form of positive reinforcement. You could even add some extra playtime after a training session if your puppy does very well.

Having your puppy's respect is also essential for successful training. If your Chihuahua respects you, it will be much easier for him to accept positive attention instead of treats because he knows you are in charge.

You may occasionally need to resort to punishment with your Chihuahua, particularly if he nips or chews on furniture. However, you have to be careful not to train him to believe in things or actions that will make your life more difficult. Never use the crate as a place to punish your Chihuahua – it should be a safe haven when your puppy wants to be alone or sleep. It is not a jail and you should not treat it as one. You can use time out instead to get your point (and disappointment) across to the puppy. Time out should be in a place that the puppy cannot interact with you, no matter how much the little guy barks, whines, or whimpers, but you should still be visible to your pup. You don't want to scare the puppy. The point is to let them know that you are still there but intentionally not interacting because of the puppy's actions. By denying him access to you without you disappearing, you are reminding him just why he needs to behave.

Photo Courtesy of
Susan Davies

Exercise – Essential but Incredibly Easy

While it can be difficult not to overfeed a Chihuahua – those large eyes can be very difficult to say no to – making sure your tiny pooch gets adequate exercise is incredibly easy. A couple of 15-minute walks by the end of the first month will be more than enough. When the weather is bad, you can simply play some games to make sure your puppy gets enough movement to be healthy. The ease of making sure a Chihuahua gets plenty of exercise is one of the reasons that so many people love them. They don't come with the traditional walks if you don't want to.

Best Activities

Chihuahuas are the perfect dog if you want a companion that can just have fun with you indoors. Apart from lounging around your home, there are a lot of games you can play with your pup.

Tidy toy is something you can do to teach your puppy to clean up toys. It's not only fun, it can help keep your home clear of dog toys. It will take some training, but it doesn't require extra treats, and as long as you go overboard on the praise, your puppy will love the attention. There are many intelligent Chihuahuas, so they will quickly learn that putting away toys will get them praise.

Find the treat is another easy game that really doesn't cost much, especially if you use Cheerios. It's also great mental stimulation. Put the treat down where your puppy can see it, then place a small cup or clean yogurt container over it. Place two identical cups or containers on either side, then switch it around. Your puppy will learn to watch the movements to figure out where the treat is. Having someone to help show what the puppy should do will help your puppy understand the point that much faster.

Other games like hide and seek, fetch, and Simon says are all things that your puppy can learn over time. With enough attention and games, you can have a very intelligent little Chihuahua that gets all the necessary exercise and excitement from easy games.

CHAPTER 8.
Housetraining

Housetraining a dog is never fun, and that is as true with Chihuahuas as it is with any other breed of canine. The difference between training a Chihuahua and most other dogs is that you really don't need to take Chihuahuas out of doors. Housetraining is essential to raising any puppy, but it is a bit easier with a breed that doesn't have to learn to go outside. With Chihuahuas, you are in for an interesting experience (although the breeder should be able to tell you about how long it took to train the parents to give you an idea of how long it could take you to complete the training with your puppy).

Two rules should be followed during this time.

1. Your puppy is not to be left to roam the house free when no one is around to monitor the puppy. Your Chihuahua won't be pleased with the idea of being in a soiled crate, so that is a deterrent from using the bathroom when you are not around.

2. Your puppy should have constant, easy access to the locations where you plan to housetrain. This is incredibly easy if you split the puppy area into a place to live and a small area where the puppy goes to the bathroom.

Once you have your training plan, be prepared to enforce all of the rules and a restroom schedule.

Understanding Your Dog

Every Chihuahua is different, so you are going to need to work with your puppy as an individual to figure out what works best with him. It may take a while before your puppy understands just what you want in those early days because it is an entirely new concept to him. If the breeder started training, you want to keep to that training though. Considering how intelligent most Chihuahuas are, if they think that they can get away with going wherever they want, it is almost always because of the people who take care of them.

HELPFUL TIP

Potty-Training Problems

Thanks to their small bladders and stubborn streaks, Chihuahuas are one of the most difficult dog breeds to house-train. You need to start house-training as soon as you bring your Chihuahua home, take it out frequently (as often as once an hour for puppies), and give your pet lots of praise and treats for doing its business outside.

Consistency is key with all dogs, no matter their personality or breed. Food is a great motivator, but you need to stick with small treats, or pieces of kibble or Cheerios to keep your puppy from overeating. As your puppy shows signs of being motivated by seeing you happy (for example, he gets excited when you do or reacts by wanting to play when you talk), start using praise as much as treats to reinforce the puppy using the bathroom in the right place.

You will need to tailor the schedule to your puppy's needs. To start with, always plan to take the puppy to the pee pad after both eating and sleeping – your puppy is almost certain to need to go after each activity. If you successfully get the puppy to the pee pad, you have a much better chance of teaching the puppy to go to the right place to do business.

Since they don't go to the bathroom outside, you really have to be vigilant with Chihuahuas. As Barbara Pendergrass of Rafina Chihuahuas explains, "Forgetting that they are housebroken happens. It's important to be diligent in watching them, and when they seem as if they are going to have an accident, picking them up and carrying them to the potty pad with no scolding helps them remember."

Housetraining should not be a scary effort, and if your Chihuahua decides that it is too much effort (even though he doesn't have to go outside), it can be frustrating. Remaining patient and kind will help convince your Chihuahua that it is worth the effort. If you stop playtime, put the

Chihuahua in a pen, and immediately clean up the mess, your Chihuahua is much more likely to decide to use the pads. Disrupting playtime or fun and having to wait for you to come back to him will not be enjoyable, and going to the bathroom on a pee pad will see like an easy way around the disruption.

Inside or Outside

Remember that you cannot send your puppy outside to use the bathroom alone. You can have netting added over a portion of your yard, but your Chihuahua should not be sent outside alone, even as an adult. Their size means that it doesn't take much of a gap or hole for them to slip through it and into unprotected areas.

It is much easier to set up areas around the home where your Chihuahua can use the bathroom. Here are a couple of recommendations from breeders about training your Chihuahua inside.

Photo Courtesy of Kristina Lesoine

1.	"During family playtime, have 2-3 piddle pads in various places of the room (especially one just outside the pen), and if the pen has a door leave it open while she/his is out playing so they can return to do their business if needed." - Linda Jangula of Chihuahuas Wee Love

2.	"They can be trained to use wee pads, doggy doors or going on a leash. Key is, they should never be left outside alone, they can be prey to wild animals and birds." - Kathy Golden of Kactus Kathy's Chihuahuas

3.	"Remember to be patient and don't expect miracles overnight! Success comes with patience and repetition." - Linda Jangula of Chihuahuas Wee Love

Establish Who Is Boss – Kind But Firm, Very Firm

As difficult as it is, you have to take a firm, consistent approach, no matter how cute the puppy is. Fight the urge to consider something good enough or close enough. Your Chihuahua needs to use the designated area and learn to hold it when inside and away from a pad. This won't happen if you make exceptions. Your Chihuahua is intelligent enough to know when you are being weak, and is going to use that as an excuse to "forget" about where to go to the bathroom.

Think of your Chihuahua's training as like that of a cat. You don't want your cat going just anywhere around the house – your Chihuahua shouldn't be free to go anywhere and everywhere either.

Positive Reinforcement – It's about Respect

Positive reinforcement works incredibly well for Chihuahuas, even the puppies. Take a few pieces of kibble or Cheerios with you when you are teaching your puppy where to go. Learning that you are the one in charge will help teach the Chihuahua to look to you for cues and instructions. They may try to push you a bit, to convince you that it's okay to let things slide because they want to enjoy time with you – not be forced to do something.

While you are being firm and consistent, when your puppy does the right thing, you have to lavish the little pup with praise. They want to hear that they are good, and if you give them an extra treat or kibble, this will put them over the moon.

Knowing what you want will make it easier for the Chihuahua to start to do things the way you want them done. By focusing on this aspect, you are establishing the respect needed for all future training.

Punishing your Chihuahua is strongly discouraged. All punishment does is to train your Chihuahua not to do something when you are around or to do it where you won't find it (at least, not until later). The lesson you are trying to teach is not the one your Chihuahua learns, so it is best to stick with positive reinforcement – that they understand very well. Training a Chihuahua (or any dog) is not exactly like teaching a human, and you cannot take the same approach.

Regular Schedule, Doggy Door, or Newspapers?

Training should pretty much be conducted inside the home because your Chihuahua cannot go outside alone safely. It is entirely possible that your Chihuahua will only go outside during walks, and that is perfectly fine since the outdoors will not be his primary place to do his business.

You do not want a doggy door for a Chihuahua because they should not be going outside on their own under any circumstances. Even if you have netting over part of the yard, there are too many ways for your wee one to escape.

It's All on You – Chihuahuas Are Among the Hardest to Housetrain

Chihuahuas love to make you happy, but they also want to do what is easiest for them. You could be in for a long training regimen when it comes to getting your Chihuahua to learn that the entire home is not a bathroom. Since they don't go outside, it is trickier to housetrain them. Regardless of how quickly your Chihuahua learns though, if you aren't firm and consistent, your dog is going to feel that inside your home is an acceptable place to use the bathroom.

Firm is not the same as mean or loud. You don't want to scare your puppy because that is going to have the opposite effect on what they learn. Kind, firm, and consistent. It does require a good bit of patience, but once your Chihuahua learns, things will get easier. Be aware that you need to make sure your Chihuahua does not "forget" either. It can be tricky, but if you don't allow exceptions, it will be a lot easier.

Anticipating Accidents

Ultimately, the best way to train a Chihuahua on where to go to the bathroom is to anticipate and act ahead of their need. Schedules are great for helping prepare for when they will go to the bathroom. After sleeping and eating are times when puppies are most likely to need to go. Playtime can also be incredibly exciting.

When your puppy is out of his area, always keep an eye out for the signs that your puppy is looking for a place to go. Your puppy shouldn't be out on its own anyway, but even while you are playing with the puppy, you should be looking for signs that your puppy needs to go to the bathroom.

CHAPTER 9.
Socialization and Experience

"It's important that a puppy socialize with other dogs of similar size and with ones that are calm and good natured. Extreme care should be taken that the puppy not be injured or frightened by a boisterous dog, even a small one."

Barbara Pendergrass
Rafina Chihuahuas

Unless properly socialized at an early age, Chihuahuas are not a particularly gregarious breed. They tend to have a great dislike for larger dogs and are incredibly wary of strangers. This is one of the reasons why they are frequently so vocal as they let the world know that they are not to be trifled with. When it comes to being around their family though, Chihuahuas can be a lot of fun, are incredibly loyal, and enjoy just lounging around. They also love to be around other Chihuahuas. If not socialized, they will be unhappy leaving their home or when people come to visit. You want your companion to be comfortable everywhere the two of you go, and that is the ultimate goal of socialization.

You will need to plan to socialize your Chihuahua because they are naturally suspicious of other people and animals. Without planning and a controlled environment, socialization can go very wrong, very quickly. If you keep things simple and under control, your Chihuahua will learn to relax and enjoy the company of other people and dogs, and not just those in the immediate family. This will mean you can take your little family member out with you when you leave home instead of always leaving your dog at home to keep down the anxiety, fear, aggression, and other negative emotions.

HELPFUL TIP
Socialization is Crucial

Chihuahuas tend to bond closely to one person and may become aggressive toward other people or dogs without proper socialization. Make sure your Chihuahua puppy gets plenty of socialization, so it doesn't turn into an "armpit piranha."

Photo Courtesy of
Elisha Jade Swanson

Benefits of Socialization

It is always important to socialize dogs, but even more so with small dogs. With a Chihuahua, socialization is absolutely essential to keep him from being a nervous wreck or an aggressive little menace. People are inclined to be overprotective and cautious when they have small dogs and puppies, and this can lead to serious problems later. Given the fact that they are the smallest of all of the dog breeds, there is an extensive history of Chihuahuas not being treated like dogs. This is part of the reason why some people have such a bad impression of them. Without proper socialization, Chihuahuas have a tendency to be either nervous or aggressive; neither of these traits is pleasant for you. Both are incredibly unhealthy for your Chihuahua.

The benefits of early socialization are that it can make things that much more enjoyable for everyone involved, no matter what the situation is. A socialized dog will approach the world from a much better place than a dog that is not socialized. A properly socialized Chihuahua can be an absolute delight to have around, something that is fantastic given that they are basically a travel-sized dog.

Problems Arising from Lack of Socialization

Socialization starts the moment your puppy arrives. Without socialization, no amount of training is going to help your Chihuahua better interact with other animals and humans. All other rules still apply during socialization, so keep that in mind while you help your dog meet new friends.

If you treat your dog like a doll or infant, protecting it from everything and everyone, the dog is going to develop small dog syndrome, particularly when you have a dog that is prone to nervousness or aggression like Chihuahuas. They need to be allowed to learn how to interact with others so that they aren't always terrified or upset with you when there are other people or dogs around them. It isn't healthy for your Chihuahua to always be anxious or nervous around others, especially when you can easily avoid it. Make time to socialize your puppy to make his life enjoyable and so that he is as happy to meet new people and dogs as you and your family are.

This is easiest to do on the short walks you take. Starting with people is the easiest path, particularly adults, because you can let them know the rules and ensure that they don't do things that could agitate or scare your puppy. Dogs may be a little scary, and your puppy is not fully vaccinated yet, which means you really shouldn't be letting your puppy get to know other canines quite yet. However, you are basically guaranteed to encounter people when you are taking a walk, which means you can start the socialization soon after your puppy arrives.

By giving your little one good experiences with other people early, your puppy will be more comfortable around strangers. This will be incredibly beneficial if you plan to take your dog out with you often or if you have company over regularly.

Small Dog Syndrome

All small dogs (not just Chihuahuas) can develop small dog syndrome if they are not properly socialized. When people say they don't like small dogs, it is almost certain it's because their experiences have been with small dogs that have not been socialized and are little terrors. It isn't life threatening, but it does mean that people are not going to want to be around your Chihuahua any more than your Chihuahua will want to have other people and dogs around it. This degrades the quality of your dog's life as well (and probably yours, too).

Photo Courtesy of
Crystal Jay Herrald-Campbell

©Crystal Herrald-Camy

The reason small dogs are prone to kind of behavior is that people tend to be overly careful with them, carrying them around instead of letting them walk, letting them get away with things because it's "cute," and thinking that the aggression isn't that big a deal. A Chihuahua cannot do nearly as much damage as a medium-sized dog, so people tend to be more dismissive of bad behavior. It is worse if you encourage it by laughing or finding it amusing.

Your Chihuahua's personality is going to be stunted if you don't act in a way that is firm and consistent. They are not babies and they can understand far more than toddlers and small children by the time they are adults. That means they are using your lack of serious training to get away with doing what they want to do. It is incredibly difficult to retrain a Chihuahua once it develops these bad behaviors.

You should always consistently apply the rules, no matter the size of your puppy and dog. As an intelligent canine, the Chihuahua learns that bad behavior will be all right from those early days if you don't apply the rules consistently. If you are protective of your puppy, that smart little dog is going to learn to fear those things. Instead of keeping your puppy isolated, let the little guy explore as much as you would a larger breed of dog. Obviously, if you are walking around your neighborhood and encounter an aggressive dog, keep your puppy away so that he doesn't correlate dogs that he meets outside his home as being a threat. Also, keep in mind that you need to walk a distance that your puppy can handle so that you aren't tempted to pick your puppy up off the ground. You can let your puppy greet friendly dogs, which you can determine by asking the people walking the strange dog. If they say it is all right, your wee friend will get a chance to sniff noses and see that other dogs are great to meet. Be prepared for your puppy to be a bit less than pleased with large dogs. If you dedicate a lot of time to socialization, it is likely that you will have a Chihuahua that views both little and big dogs about the same instead of discriminating against larger breeds.

Why Genetics Matter

Genetics are important in terms of not only the dog's health but their personality. Given the wide range of potential personalities, you want to get a dog that has parents with a similar temperament to what you want in your dog. Early socialization can help bring out a love for new people, dogs, and experiences. You will want to learn whether or not your puppy's parents are skittish or standoffish so you will know what to expect and can watch for those traits and correct them as early as possible.

Knowing the parents' personalities will help you plan for training too. If one parent tends to be shy or active, you can plan to play to the strengths and weaknesses noted by the breeder.

Common Problems

This is a breed that is notorious for being either very outspoken or terrified. These are definitely the extremes, but it is possible that without socialization, you could have these problems with your dog.

One of the biggest problems reported with Chihuahuas is aggressiveness toward other dogs, particularly large ones. They may also be aggressive toward people, which can be a serious problem if they start nipping and biting. Most of these symptoms are of small dog syndrome, but Chihuahuas naturally do not like larger dogs. Since there aren't any dogs smaller than this breed, you can expect that without proper socialization your Chihuahua will develop an aggressive posture to most dogs he meets.

On a much smaller scale, Chihuahuas are notorious barkers. Even if they aren't aggressive or unfriendly, you may find that your Chihuahua just doesn't know when to shut up. The smallest noise can set your dog off, but a knock at the door will send him into fits. Training your Chihuahua to be less obnoxious will help make your 15 to 20 years together a lot more enjoyable.

Properly Greeting New People

There are typically two reactions by people encountering Chihuahuas – either they will be excited and want to play or they will be annoyed and pass by without looking at your dog. If your dog is very vocal, you will get a lot more of the latter reaction.

It is the stranger who comes up wanting to play with your puppy that is going to be the bigger problem. It is possible that some people will not understand proper etiquette and will try to pick up your Chihuahua. People who act without getting approval first should be avoided if they don't listen when you explain that your puppy should not be held.

The same rules apply out of the house as inside – let your puppy initiate the interaction. Strangers can get low and hold out a hand, but the little dog should approach them, not the other way around. You want the experience to be fun and exciting for your young four-legged friend. This means things should be on the puppy's terms so that he doesn't feel like he is being overwhelmed or that what he wants doesn't matter. By initiating contact, the puppy will develop a sense of comfort when he is outside of the home.

Behavior Around Other Dogs

There are plenty of Chihuahuas that live in homes with other dogs, both large and small. With proper socialization, your Chihuahua can learn that large dogs are fun to have around, and it is even easier if you have big friendly dogs at home.

If you don't have other dogs, you will find it more challenging. In the beginning, your chihuahua should not be exposed to other dogs until it has completed its shots. This means actively avoiding dogs outside your home. You will want to do this in a way that does not give your puppy the impression that it is because the other dog is dangerous. As soon are your puppy has received all of the shots, ask friends to have play dates with their dogs (if their dogs are friendly). There may be a delay in socialization with other dogs, so that makes it all the more important to get started as soon as possible. You want your Chihuahua to be comfortable leaving the home, and that will be nearly impossible if the little guy doesn't have positive experiences with other dogs.

Some breeders also recommend that you have at least two Chihuahuas at a time. Chihuahuas don't have the same aversion to their own breed as some other breeds, and having a second Chihuahua means that you won't feel guilty about leaving your dog at home alone. This can reduce his anxiety and give him someone to play with when there aren't any people around.

CHAPTER 10.
Being a Puppy Parent

Having a puppy as a pet can be incredibly fun and exciting. At the same time, it is unbelievably tiring and frustrating. A puppy brings a whole new perspective to the world that people simply do not see without a puppy's guidance. This is what makes it seem difficult to see him as the destructive little creature he can be.

When it comes to Chihuahuas, this relationship is compounded by the fact that your puppy can be willful, and with his intellect, any exception to the rules will be remembered and exploited for a long time. If he senses any hesitation, he is smart enough to know how to exploit it. If you decide that something is close enough, he is going to exploit that. Your Chihuahua is very attuned to you and your attitude, and if you show any weakness toward making him do what he should do, he will manipulate that in the future, looking for ways to duplicate your decision to let something go.

When properly trained, Chihuahuas are an incredible companion. It just takes a lot of work in those early days to ensure he learns the right habits.

Photo Courtesy of
Crystal Jay Herrald-Campbell

Staying Consistently Firm

When it comes to training a Chihuahua, you must be firm and consistent. Over the course of his life, your Chihuahua is going to try to get away with misbehavior, not out of rebellion, but just to see if he can. It is one of the main reasons why you really cannot make exceptions to the rules for him, not even while he is still a puppy.

If you get accustomed to making exceptions because the puppy is adorable, you are not going to succeed in training your Chihuahua. He may be small, but he can be very sharp. He is intelligent and can be quite stubborn in trying to get his way. You must be unyielding with your puppy if you want a well-behaved dog.

Your dog does not mean any harm and certainly is not trying to be rebellious. Chihuahuas simply like to have things their way, and they are generally clever enough to get it. However, it could mean your puppy does not respect you. That is why it is so important to be consistent and firm. Your dog has to know that you are the alpha of the pack at all times.

Puppy Gnawing and What to Watch For

DID YOU KNOW?
**Small Dogs,
Big Damage**

According to British insurance agency PayingTooMuch, Chihuahuas are the most destructive dog breed, responsible for an average of $1,300 in damage over the course of their lifetime from chewing, scratching, staining, digging, and ripping.

Puppies gnaw. At first, they are teething and it feels good to sink their teeth into something. Later, they do it as part of their learning and socialization. Chihuahuas are one of the breeds that you must be particularly careful with because they have a tendency to be destructive when they are bored. Gnawing on things is part of a habit or to let you know that he doesn't like being left alone. Since your puppy is so small, he can get into a lot of places to gnaw on things that he absolutely shouldn't. This is one reason why your little guy should not be allowed outside of his puppy area without supervision.

For the first few months after your puppy comes home, you should keep the pup secured in a place where there are only a few things to chew on. You also need to make sure there is not a way for your puppy to escape his area. That means making sure there is no furniture or objects that can be moved or knocked around and jumped up on. He will start problem solving remarkably early, and while he will not be prone to knocking down gates and boundaries, he is not averse to finding ways around them.

When your puppy is not in the enclosed space, you must keep an eye on him at all times. Just like when you are taking care of an infant or toddler, once you turn to look away, that puppy is going to be getting into things that he or she shouldn't be getting into. If you do not have time to keep an eye on your Chihuahua, keep the puppy in a place where there is not much to chew on (besides the things you don't mind the puppy chewing up).

You can keep toys and chewing toys around your puppy at all times, particularly in the Chihuahua's designated area. This helps the puppy learn what is appropriate to chew. Once it is time to come out and play, your Chihuahua will learn what not to chew, which is why you must keep your focus on the puppy. Over time, your dog will learn the things that are acceptable to use as a chew toy.

Possible Problems with Chihuahuas

"One of the most unwanted behaviors is the aggressive barking that some owners deal with on a regular basis."

Linda Jangula
Chihuahuas Wee Love

Besides aggression, one of the biggest complaints people have about Chihuahuas is that they bark a lot. Finding out about the parents can help you determine the probability of it being a problem with your puppy. However, you should plan to train your pup not to bark incessantly, even if the parents are relatively quiet. In all likelihood, the parents were

Photo Courtesy of
Kayleigh Denyer

trained not to bark, so it may not be a personality trait so much as very good training. Make sure to ask the trainer. This is also why socialization is so important.

To deter constant barking, you can use a water gun when he starts barking. Similar to the way to deter cats, a Chihuahua usually doesn't like the surprise of a shot of water to his body. Do be careful not to get his or her ears wet.

Linda Jangula warns of another problem as well: "Another issue that is like the one that many other breeds have is making or wetting in the house. Since these little ones are so close to the floor or carpet, it may be difficult to see when they are marking which allows for a habit to form before the owner even realizes it." You will need to constantly watch your puppy, particularly the males. If you notice that your puppy is not following the housetraining rules, you may need to deter your puppy's desire to mark your home by getting a diaper wrap.

Besides issues with barking and housetraining, Chihuahua are notorious for eating feces. Since they are close to the ground, they are able to snatch up poop before you even notice it is there. It's really gross and can be difficult to discourage if you don't have a constant eye on your Chihuahua while you are out walking. You will need to remain vigilant even after your Chihuahua becomes an adult. It's a habit that he can pick

Photo Courtesy of
Donna Bass

up after he is no longer a puppy because the smell is just too tempting, especially if you go near places where water fowl spend time. Fortunately, you don't need to spend much time outside with the little one, which can make it a lot easier to help him refrain from this disgusting behavior.

Playtime!

Playtime is awesome for you and the puppy. Chihuahuas just want to be with their pack having a good time, and you are giving it everything it needs to stay out of trouble. Not to mention that a Chihuahua is so incredibly cute as a puppy that it is hardly a chore to play with him until he is too tired to do much.

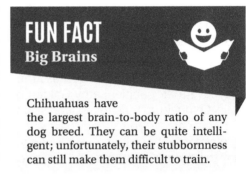

FUN FACT
Big Brains

Chihuahuas have the largest brain-to-body ratio of any dog breed. They can be quite intelligent; unfortunately, their stubbornness can still make them difficult to train.

Make time in the schedule for regular playtime. No matter how busy you are, this is something that you need to do several times a day to properly train your Chihuahua. He will not like to be alone, and this is the period of time when he can really start to understand the rules and boundaries. You can train him over the course of his entire life, but what you teach him now will have a huge effect on how well you can train him as he matures and afterward. Remember, this is the foundation for all of your puppy's later training.

Start teaching the puppy tricks as early as possible too. This not only keeps your Chihuahua's mind working, it can help you bond. It is a remarkably enjoyable way to engage the Chihuahua in physical and mental stimulation that will reduce the tendency to chew and destroy everything nearby.

Chihuahuas love to be with you, and your puppy will want to impress you with what he can do. Taking him places to explore and be active is the pinnacle of the best life to a Chihuahua. Playing with your puppy provides a safe and fun environment to learn how to behave. Your dedication now will equate to an adorable, loving, loyal companion for a long time.

CHAPTER 11.
Living with Other Dogs

Chihuahua puppies are much more likely to get along with your current dog or dogs than an adult Chihuahua. That does not mean that they will be entirely accepting of your other dogs, but you can treat it as an easy way to start socializing with them once your puppy has gotten all of the necessary shots.

Chihuahuas do prefer to have company, but most breeders recommend having another Chihuahua because they love other Chihuahuas as much as they love their people. Kathy Golden of Kactus Kathy's Chihuahuas puts it well: "Chihuahuas tend to be clannish and are not fond of other breeds, especially big dogs." If you already have a dog, this can help your Chihuahua start to overcome those biases. However, you will need to go about it the right way to let your Chihuahua and dog become comfortable with each other.

Photo Courtesy of
Karen Moore

Introducing Your New Puppy

The introductions need to start in a neutral place because your dog may feel territorial. Neutral ground will make your dog feel more at ease with the new puppy since the new Chihuahua is not invading your dog's space. It doesn't matter what the puppy is, this is always true when introducing a new dog into your home.

As your puppy and dog (or dogs) begin to feel comfortable around each other, you can start to make your way back home. When they all enter the home together, there will already be some familiarity between your puppy and the rest of your pack.

> **HELPFUL TIP**
> **Stick With Chihuahuas**
>
> More than any other dog breed, Chihuahuas tend to prefer hanging out with other Chihuahuas and become aggressive toward other dog breeds. It's not impossible to introduce a Chihuahua to your existing family dog, but you should be aware that it may be a slow, difficult introduction.

This sense of familiarity is not an inseparable bond. You will need to keep the puppy and your other dogs separated when you are not around. The puppy should have some space where only he or she can rest. This was part of the initial prep work, so by the time your puppy comes into the home, this area should already be established.

There should be nothing in the puppy's area that belongs to your other dogs. Not having a separate area can create unnecessary tension and problems that are not likely to be resolved peacefully. Your Chihuahua will want to chew on everything, and the concept of possessions doesn't really mean anything quite yet. However, your dog will see it as a challenge to his or her place, and may act accordingly. This is also true when your puppy is out of the designated area. You need to make sure there is nothing that belongs to your other dog within the puppy's reach. All you have to do is store the toys when it is time for the puppy to play.

Feeding time should take place in different locations around the home. Food is one of the biggest causes of jealousy, and you do not want any kind of unnecessary tension between your puppy and your current pets. It may be possible to move the bowls closer together later to make feeding time easier, but at least in the beginning you should keep them separated.

Dogs get jealous when they see their people giving attention to other dogs, even puppies. Be prepared for this when you bring the puppy

Photo Courtesy of Joanna Elliker

home. You will need to make sure your dog continues to get one-on-one time with you so that he or she does not feel like the puppy is a replacement. Make sure you already have established rules and schedules so that you can give your other dog enough attention on a daily basis. You will need to be firm and consistent with your puppy and your dog.

One of the biggest benefits of having a dog is that your dog is very likely to automatically start to scold your puppy when your puppy misbehaves. Your dog is not going to feel the same fit of adoration looking at the puppy, making your dog a great mentor and teacher for the Chihuahua puppy. While you cannot rely on the dog to be the primary trainer of your Chihuahua, it does help the puppy understand where he or she is in the pack and that certain behaviors are not acceptable. You need to let your dog do the scolding and reprimanding, but do make sure that the puppy is not being harmed. Thinking of your dog as a babysitter can help you establish the right balance in how the dog and puppy interact.

If your dog does not assume a role like this, that is also all right. You don't want to try to force a role on your dog with the new puppy. The canines will figure it out if you just give them time and supervise them until it is established.

Inside-Dog Mentality

Since Chihuahuas are not able to go outside without supervision, they are one of the few breeds that stay inside most of their lives. It gives them a different perspective of the world. This can also make them a bit more protective of their space if they are not properly socialized. If you already have a dog, your dog can help your Chihuahua feel more comfortable, but it could also be problematic if you let your dog out, but not the Chihuahua. Not only could the Chihuahua get jealous of the smells it is not getting to experience, your dog could get jealous about having to go outside in rain, sleet, or other unpleasant weather. You will need to keep an eye on this to keep the peace between your dogs. Your Chihuahua is going to have a very different understanding of the world since most of its very long life will be spent inside the home.

Biting, Fighting, and Puppy Anger Management

Puppies are a handful for many reasons, but this can be one of the most challenging problems in dealing with a young dog. Chihuahuas are known for being pretty even-tempered, but you do have to watch the puppy when he is young. There will be times when the puppy is not happy, and the result may be nipping and lashing out at your other dog. This is quite likely when your Chihuahua puppy reaches an adult size.

Photo Courtesy of
Tasha Snitch

Firm and consistent is the only way to deal with this problem.

An untrained Chihuahua can actually be a pretty monstrous dog. This is a breed that requires training to fight the urge to force other dogs to do things a certain way.

You do need to spend a lot of time with the puppy as well so that you can understand when it is being playful and when it is upset. When you spot aggressive behavior (not just play), you have to immediately step in and train your Chihuahua that this is unacceptable behavior.

Starting training at a very early stage can help you see when your puppy is being playful, and when the behavior goes a little further than being playful.

Raising Multiple Puppies at Once

Since many breeders recommend having more than one Chihuahua at one time, you may decide to go ahead and get more than one puppy in the beginning. Raising one puppy is nearly a full-time job, but there are some who take to raising two at a time. If you want to raise two Chihuahua puppies at the same time, you are definitely in for a challenge. These dogs are nobody's fool, and when they put their brains together, you are going to have a hard time outsmarting them. You are going to have to really work to get them to behave the way you want them to once they reach maturity.

One of the first things you will notice that disappears is your personal life. You are going to be tending to your puppies the vast majority of your day. This is absolutely essential if you do not want to have twice the destruction in your home.

First, you have to spend time with them together, and you will have to give each of them alone time with you. They are not the same dog, so you cannot treat them that way. Each puppy will have different strengths and weaknesses. Spending time with them together is easy, but you must take time with each of them on their own as well. It will be a challenge, especially as one whines as you play with the other. One of the best ways to deal with this is to have someone else play with the other puppy, then to switch. This keeps both puppies happily occupied so that they don't get jealous of each other.

Just as your puppy is likely to fight with an older dog, the Chihuahua puppies are almost certainly going to start fighting when they are between three and six months old. They are establishing which of them is the dominant dog, and that is fine. You just need to make sure they understand that you are the alpha of the pack so that they do not start to question your authority over them.

Just as you need to minimize the puppies' distractions (and they will be their own worst distractions), you have to minimize your own. If you are preparing their food, you need to stay focused on that until the puppies are eating. If you are getting ready for a walk, as soon as you get the leashes on, get out of the door. The puppies are watching and learning, so show them how to stay focused and follow through. If you do not, you have no one to blame but yourself when they start to get rowdy and unmanageable while they are waiting. After all, you got them excited about eating or walking, only to leave them waiting. Dogs do not understand the concept of patience, but with all of that excitement now pent up and ready to burst, you are going to be the one to suffer for failing to follow through with the next activity.

Remember, their misbehavior is really a reflection of how you have trained them. If you constantly require them to focus during training, but you fail to focus on doing tasks with them, both of your puppies are going to notice. Be consistent and focused to avoid many unnecessary issues with your puppies.

If you find you cannot decide if you want a second Chihuahua, you can get one Chihuahua puppy and one of another breed. It is very likely you will find that the dogs end up being pretty similar, highlighting how training, environment, and attention play a large role in how the puppy grows up. Or you may find that your two dogs have very different and distinct personalities. It is certainly an interesting experiment that can give you something to watch for years. And it will give you a much better understanding of the breed.

Photo Courtesy of Claire Borg

CHAPTER 12.
Training Your Chihuahua Puppy

Chihuahuas are able to figure things out much faster than some small dogs. Despite a lot of energy and a desire to enjoy their time with you, training a Chihuahua is probably going to be easier than with many other small dogs (though not as easy as with working dogs and really intelligent breeds). You may have to work through the sort of being headstrong bit because Chihuahuas can be stubborn. However, with a firm and consistent approach, your Chihuahua will learn to respect and listen to you.

Working with a cute, energetic puppy can be tiring. By making sure to follow through with a few actions, you will find that your Chihuahua will pick up on the training much quicker. Keep in mind that training your puppy is a long-term commitment. Even if your Chihuahua isn't rebellious, the puppy probably just wants to have fun. Your puppy won't want to anger you, but gentle begging and puppy eyes can be very effective, and Chihuahuas will learn that, particularly if you give in during a training session.

Given how small the dog is, even as an adult, many people will always think of their Chihuahua as puppies – it's incredibly difficult not to think that way. If you consider how intelligent your Chihuahua is, you are actually doing your pup a great disservice by not training as early as possible. Intelligent dogs need to use their brains to keep them from boredom and destructive behavior.

Photo Courtesy of
Carrie- Anne Selwyn

Firm and Consistent

There are many times in life where you will feel something is "close enough." This is never a good idea with an intelligent dog. He will study his people and figure out ways to get what he wants with as little work as possible. Wanting to please you will still drive a Chihuahua, but if you are willing to give an inch, your puppy will take it and see how much further you can be pushed. Exceptions and leniency are seen by your puppy as having some control over the situation, and that is not something you want him to learn when he is young. It just makes it that much harder to make him take you seriously later.

HELPFUL TIP
Positive Reinforcement is Key

Chihuahuas can be extremely stubborn and difficult to train. They do best with positive reinforcement—be sure to give your pet plenty of praise and treats when it does what you ask. Yelling at a Chihuahua can make it nervous and can cause it to become fear aggressive, so refrain from hollering when your Chihuahua piddles in your house.

Keeping a consistent and firm approach during training will make life for easier for you and your puppy. Even if you are tired at the end of a long day at work, you have to enforce the rules. No matter how cute or friendly your puppy is being, you must make sure that all of the rules you have been teaching remain firmly in place. If you don't feel up to it, have a family member do the training. If you don't have anyone to help you, you can change up the training a bit to make it more enjoyable. It is fine to change things up if you are having a rough time, as long as you remain consistent. Interacting with your Chihuahua can make for a much more enjoyable experience, and can even cheer you up. Consistency and firmness do not mean that you have to do the same thing all the time. You just need to make sure that your puppy understands that you are in charge and there is no negotiating on that. This will keep your puppy on the right track to being a great companion instead of a little dictator.

If everyone in your family participates in training, you need to make sure everyone is on the same page. Stephanie Lucas of Lucas Chihuahuas says, "Be consistent. Teach everyone in the family to use the same words and tell them not to say them unless they have the time to follow through. If you say 'out' they go out. It's not a question. A well-trained dog is a loved dog and less likely to be surrendered to a pound someday."

Ultimately, your Chihuahua's success is your own success. Everything your dog learns to do successfully is because you were firm and consistent when it came time to train.

Gain Respect Early

Photo Courtesy of Ramona Kleespies

Being firm and consistent in your approach to training will start gaining you respect from your little canine early in your relationship. This is something you will need to keep building over time. Without respect, your Chihuahua is going to think you don't mean what you say, and will start to try to get his own way. As long as you are firm and consistent, respect should be a natural part of the bond. That means that you cannot multi-task while you are training your puppy, or even just playing with your puppy. The Chihuahua wants your full attention and will find a way to get it, even if it means breaking the rules to get your attention.

Positive reinforcement is the best way to gain respect, particularly if you use positive interaction. Playing and training your puppy every day helps build a healthy, positive relationship that will teach your puppy where he or she fits into the pack. Your puppy learns that it is part of the family, but that you are the one in charge.

Operant Conditioning Basics

Operant conditioning is the scientific term for actions and consequences. What you have to do is provide your Chihuahua puppy with the right consequences for each behavior.

The best way to use operant conditioning is through positive reinforcement, particularly since the Chihuahua is so attached to people. This type of training is more effective with working dogs and dogs that have a long history with people because they want to please their people. They want to work with you and fulfill their tasks. Knowing that they are doing something right does a lot more to encourage their behavior than knowing when they do something wrong. With so much energy, they will be able to keep trying until they get it right.

There are two types of reinforcements for operant conditioning:

- Primary reinforcements
- Secondary reinforcements

You will use both during your Chihuahua's training.

Primary Reinforcements

A primary reinforcement gives your dog something that it needs to survive, like food or social interaction. Both of these can be effective for training your Chihuahua – he loves spending time with you and may be happy to have treats. That is exactly what makes treats so effective during training.

Initially, you will rely on primary reinforcements since you do not have to teach your Chihuahua to enjoy them. However, you have to keep a balance. Mealtime and playtime should never be denied to your puppy, no matter how poorly the puppy performs. These things are essential to living, and you will have to give them the essentials – that is not negotiable. It is things like treats and extra playtime that you use to reinforce good behavior.

Err on providing too much attention and affection over too many treats. Because of their small stature, Chihuahuas need to keep a well-balanced diet to be healthy. If you rely on treats instead of attention, you are setting yourself and your pup up for serious problems later.

Secondary Reinforcements

You used repetition to get good at your hobbies, sports, and other physical activities – this is secondary reinforcement. Without a doubt, Pavlov's experiment with dogs is the most recognizable example of secondary reinforcement. Using the bell, Pavlov taught the test dogs that when the bell rang it meant it was time to eat. The dogs began to associate the ringing of a bell to meal time. They were conditioned to associate something with a primary reinforcement. You can see this in your home when you use a can opener. If you have any cats or dogs, they probably come running as soon as the can opener starts going.

Secondary reinforcements work because your Chihuahua will associate the trigger with something that is required. This makes your puppy more likely to do as you tell it to do. Dogs that are taught to sit using a treat only will automatically react by sitting down when you have a treat

Photo Courtesy of
Rayne Music

in your hand. They won't even wait for you to tell them to sit. They know that sitting means more food, so they automatically do it once you make that association. Of course, this is not the proper training because they need to learn to sit when you say sit, and not when you have a treat. That is the real challenge.

Fortunately, it is relatively easy to train a Chihuahua puppy with the right trigger because Chihuahuas can be both intelligent and eager to please. While your puppy may enjoy food, you can show him that the trigger is the word, not the food. He may get it much faster than many other dog breeds.

You can also use toys and attention as a way of getting your Chihuahua to do the right thing. If you have a regular schedule and you are willing to change it a little to give your puppy a little extra attention for doing something right, that will be just as effective as a treat because they love attention. You can take the pup on an extra walk, spend a little more time playing with a favorite toy, or take some time to cuddle with the puppy.

Sometimes punishment is required too, but you need to be very careful about how you do it. Trying to punish a Chihuahua can be tricky, but denying your Chihuahua attention can work very well. Simply put your puppy in a penned off area where the Chihuahua can see you but cannot interact with you. The little guy will whine and whimper to let you know that he or she wants out. Don't give in because this is the punishment. Just ignore your puppy to teach the lesson about proper behavior.

Punishments must happen right after the event. If your Chihuahua chews something up and you don't find out for several hours, it is too late to punish the puppy. The same is true for rewards. To reinforce behavior, the reward or punishment must be given almost immediately. When you praise or punish your puppy, make sure you keep eye contact. You can also take the puppy by the scruff of the neck to ensure that you keep eye contact. You won't need to do that when you are praising your pooch because he or she will automatically keep eye contact. Chihuahuas can be absolutely driven by hearing your praise.

Why Food Is a Bad Reinforcement Tool

The small Chihuahua stature means that food is not something you should use often as a reward. As your Chihuahua ages his metabolism will slow, and since he cannot go for long walks, it is difficult to help him work off the extra calories. It does not take much for a Chihuahua to become overweight. Keep in mind that he should only be about 6 pounds. With affection and attention being such successful motivators, it is best to use them as much as possible instead of getting your Chihuahua accustomed to treats for rewards. Use treats sparingly.

Another reason to use treats sparingly is because you don't want your puppy to respond to you primarily when you have food. If your Chihuahua associates training with treats, you may have a difficult time training your Chihuahua to listen to you without them. Given how difficult a Chihuahua can be to housetrain, you really don't want him to only go when you have treats. If your pup learns to do what you say, these kinds of problems should be reduced.

Treats can be used in the early stages when your puppy's metabolism is high and has not been conditioned to respond to secondary reinforcement. This will give you something to help your puppy learn to focus as you train him to understand other incentives. It should not take too long before you can start transitioning away from treats as a reinforcement tool. Treats are also the best way of training certain types of behavior, such as rolling over. Your puppy will automatically follow the treat, making it easy to understand what you mean.

Treats are also best for the beginning commands (sit, stay, and leave it). Your dog does not understand words yet, and will quickly make the

Photo Courtesy of
Barbara Pendergrass
Rafina Chihuahuas

connection between what you are saying and why the treat is being offered. Leave it is very difficult to teach without treats because there is no incentive to drop something if your puppy really wants the object already in his or her mouth. Treats are something that will make the puppy drop whatever is in the puppy's mouth as the attention and desire focuses on food.

Small Steps to Success

The first few weeks, or maybe even the first couple of months, are a time with a very steep learning curve. Your puppy is not going to understand what you are doing in the beginning as you try to convince your little Chihuahua to use the bathroom in a certain area. The best way to train the puppy is to realize that you need to start slow – don't begin with expectations that your puppy will be housetrained in a week (that won't happen). Your puppy must learn the daily routine (which you will be doing at the same time). Once the schedule and environment are less exciting, your Chihuahua will have an easier time focusing during training sessions.

Training should begin from day 1. Even through your puppy is just getting to know the environment, you need to start putting some of the rules in place. As your puppy gets familiar with you and the environment, you can teach the Chihuahua about its area and that the crate is for sleeping. Learning to go into the crate on command has some obvious benefits, particularly if you leave home every day. This is when you start using treats to train the puppy to go into the crate and do other basic activities.

Starting from day 1 does not mean trying to do everything – you must start small. Give treats for little things that your puppy might do anyway, like explore the crate. Once your Chihuahua starts to understand the reward system, training will start to get easier.

Training Options

Chihuahuas can be very difficult because they are cute and good at getting what they want. It can be a lot more difficult to be strong enough to enforce your rules. Having a trainer can help both you and your Chihuahua. The trainer can let you know where you are going wrong and help your puppy get the basics down.

If you have an adult Chihuahua, you will want to consider getting a trainer for any current problems, particularly aggression and bad housetraining. Your trainer can help correct the problems, showing you how to do it without going about it the wrong way. Chihuahuas are a unique breed, so unless you have experience with training dogs, getting a trainer can be incredibly beneficial.

CHAPTER 13.
Basic Commands

Photo Courtesy of
Shayla –Tiah Winch

Not all Chihuahuas are good at learning tricks, but if you start when your Chihuahua is a puppy, you are guaranteed to get at least the basics ingrained into their minds. Kathy Golden of Kactus Kathy's Chihuahuas recommends getting an early start: "They are not any more difficult than other breeds to train. Start training early!" If you have seen poorly behaved Chihuahua, it is a sign that their people did not bother to train them, not that they are bad dogs. Considering how intelligent many of them are, spending time training them can be something you enjoy together, acting like a comedy duo for years to come. If you don't start early, your Chihuahua is not going to take you as seriously because they are not accustomed to following commands.

There is also a very good chance that your Chihuahua can become quite the little entertainer. Many of them are quite intelligent, so training them to do more can help keep them from getting bored. It also significantly increases the odds that your Chihuahua will be able to learn more advanced tricks later. By establishing the training relationship early, your Chihuahua will learn to listen and understand what will result in those delicious treats.

Why Size, Life Span, and Personality Make Them Ideal Companions

Training is something that is a lot of fun with a Chihuahua. They can be incredibly intelligent, and training them makes them even more fun to spend time with. When properly trained they can be one of the best companions because they can travel with you anywhere you go. Since they can live up to 20 years, completed training will last for a very long time, making it a lot of fun just to chill or show off how smart your little guy is. If a Chihuahua is well trained, the people around you will have a great time watching your travel-sized buddy show off that sharp intellect. Since they can go with you virtually anywhere, training will quickly pay off as you and your best friend share some of the most memorable lessons. If your Chihuahua is not trained, it will be much harder to take your canine places as your Chihuahua will be wary of strangers and is much more likely to be aggressive. It isn't cute when they are full-grown adults barking at people when you are just trying to enjoy a little time away from home.

HELPFUL TIP
Small Dog Syndrome

Also called "Napoleon Syndrome," Small Dog Syndrome is overly aggressive behavior from little dogs. This is often the result of small breeds who aren't treated like dogs. Teach your Chihuahua basic commands and require it to walk on a leash from time to time to help it understand that it's a dog and not your purse protector.

Picking the Right Reward

One of the most interesting aspects of having a Chihuahua is determining the right reward. You want to keep the treats to a minimum but that should be fine with a Chihuahua since there are so many other things that can motivate them. Treats may be a good starting point, but you will need to quickly switch to something that is a secondary reinforcer. Praise, additional playtime, and extra petting are all fantastic rewards for Chihuahua pets since they care about how you feel and your reaction to them. Plopping down to watch a movie and letting the puppy sit with you will be a great reward after an intense training session. Not only did your puppy learn, but you both now get to relax and enjoy just chilling together.

If you begin to gain the respect of your Chihuahua, that can be used to help train your dog. At the end of each session, give your puppy extra attention or a nice walk to demonstrate how pleased you are with the progress that has been made.

Successful Training

Training is about learning the commands. If your Chihuahua learns to respond only to the rewards (such as the dog that sits as soon as you have a treat in your hand), the training was not successful.

Gaining the respect of your dog is generally the key in being a successful trainer, but with a Chihuahua it also means dedicated attention – you have all of the puppy's attention during a training session. As you and your Chihuahua work together, your dog will come to respect you (so long as you remain consistent and firm). Do not expect respect in the early days of training because your puppy does not have the understanding or relationship required to be able to understand. Fortunately, their intelligence will start to show early on, making it easy to see when they are starting to respond to you instead of just the reward. This is the time when you can start switching to rewards that are fun instead of those that center around treats and food.

Even in the beginning, you need to make handling and petting a part of the reward. Although your dog does not quite understand it for what it is, your Chihuahua will begin to understand that treats and petting are both types of rewards. This will make it easier to switch from treats to a more attention-based reward system. Associating handling and petting as being enjoyable will also encourage your puppy to look at playtime as a great reward. No matter how much they love to eat, being entertained and playing with you will be a welcome reward since it means the puppy is not alone or bored.

Basic Commands

For the Chihuahua, there are five basic commands that you must teach them, and ones that you will probably want to start training your puppy to understand. These commands are the basis for a happy and enjoyable relationship as your Chihuahua learns how to behave. By the time your puppy learns the five commands, the purpose of training will be clear to your Chihuahua. That will make it much easier to train them on the more complex concepts.

You should train the puppy in the order of the list as well. Sit is a basic command, and sitting is something all dogs as well as your Chihuahua already do. Teaching leave it and how to bark less are both difficult and fight the instincts and desires of your Chihuahua pooch. They are going to take longer to learn than the other commands, so you want to have the necessary tools already in place to increase your odds of success.

Here are some basic guidelines to follow during training.

- Everyone in the home should be a part of the Chihuahua training because the Chihuahua needs to learn to listen to everyone in the household, and not just one or two people.
- To get started, select an area where you and your puppy have no distractions, including noise. Leave your phone and other devices out of range so that you keep your attention on the puppy.
- Stay happy and excited about the training. Your puppy will pick up on your enthusiasm, and will focus better because of it.
- Start to teach sit when your puppy is around eight weeks old.
- Be consistent and firm as you teach.
- Bring a special treat to the first few training sessions, such as chicken or cheese.

Once you are prepared, you can get started working and bonding with your cute little Chihuahua.

Sit

Once you settle into your quiet training location with the special treat, begin the training. It is relatively easy to train your dog to obey this command. Wait until your puppy starts to sit down and say sit as he or she sits. If your puppy finishes sitting down, start to give praise for it. Naturally, this will make your puppy incredibly excited and wiggly, so it may take a bit of time before he or she will want to sit again. When the time comes and the puppy starts to sit again, repeat the process.

It is going to take more than a couple of sessions for the puppy to fully connect your words with the actions. In fact, it could take a little over a week for your puppy to get it. Chihuahuas are intelligent, but at this age there is still so much to learn that the puppy will have a hard time focusing. Commands are something completely new to your little companion. However, once your puppy understands your intention and masters sit, the other commands will likely be a little bit easier to teach.

Once your puppy has demonstrated a mastery over sit, it is time to start teaching down.

Down

Repeat the same process to teach this command as you did for sit. Wait until the puppy starts to lie down, then say the word. If the Chihuahua finishes the action, offer your chosen reward.

It will probably take a little less time to teach this command after you start training it.

Wait until your puppy has mastered down before moving on to stay.

Stay

This command is going to be more difficult since it isn't something that your puppy does naturally. Be prepared for "stay" to take a bit longer to train. It is also important that your dog has mastered and will consistently sit and lie down on command before you start to teach stay.

Choose which of these two commands you want to use to get started, and then you will need to be consistent. Once your dog understands stay for either sit or down, you can train with the second command. Just make sure the first position is mastered before trying the second.

Tell your puppy to either sit or stay. As you do this, place your hand in front of the puppy's face. Wait until the puppy stops trying to lick your hand before you begin again.

When the puppy settles down, take a step away from the Chihuahua. If your puppy is not moving, say stay and give the puppy the treat and some praise for staying.

Giving the reward to your puppy indicates that the command is over, but you also need to indicate that the command is complete. The puppy has to learn to stay until you say it is okay to leave the spot. Once you give the okay to move, do not give treats. Come should not be used as the okay word as it is a command used for something else.

Repeat these steps, taking more steps further away from the puppy after a successful command.

Once your puppy understands stay when you move away, start training to stay even if you are not moving. Extend the amount of time required for the puppy to stay in one spot so that he or she understands that stay ends with the okay command.

When you feel that your puppy has stay mastered, start to train the puppy to come.

Come

This is the last in the series of commands since you cannot teach this one until the puppy has learned the previous commands. The first two commands do not require the puppy to know other commands to get started (it is just easier to train if the puppy already has an understanding of what commands are and how the puppy is expected to react to them).

Photo Courtesy of Cheryl Grange

Before you start, decide if you want to use come or come here for the command. You will need to be consistent in the words you use, so make sure you plan it so that you will intentionally use the right command every time.

Leash the puppy.

Tell the puppy to stay. Move away from the puppy.

Say the command you will use for come and give a gently tug on the leash toward you. As long as you did not use the term to indicate that the stay command was done, your puppy will begin to understand the purpose of your new command. If you used the term to indicate the end of stay, it will confuse your puppy because the Chihuahua will associate the command with being able to move freely.

Repeat these steps, building a larger distance between you and the puppy. Once the puppy seems to get it, remove the leash and start at a close distance. If your puppy does not seem to understand the command, give some visual clues about what you want. For example, you can pat your leg or snap your fingers. As soon as your puppy comes running over to you, offer a reward.

Leave It

This is going to be one of the most difficult commands you will teach your puppy because it goes against both your puppy's instincts and interests. Your puppy wants to keep whatever he or she has, so you are going to have to offer something better. It is essential to teach it early though, as your Chihuahua is going to be very destructive in the early days. You want to get the trigger in place to convince the puppy to drop things.

You may need to start teaching this command outside of the training arena as it has a different starting point.

Photo Courtesy of
Margaret Scott

Start when you have time to dedicate yourself to the lesson. You have to wait until the puppy has something in his or her mouth to drop. Toys are usually best. Offer the puppy a special treat. As the Chihuahua drops the toy, say leave it, and hand over the treat.

This is going to be one of those rare times when you must use a treat because your puppy needs something better to convince him or her to drop the toy. For now, your puppy needs that incentive, something more tempting than what he or she already has before your puppy can learn the command.

This will be one of the two commands that will take the longest to teach (quiet being the other). Be prepared to be patient with your pup. Once your puppy gets it, start to teach leave it with food. This is incredibly important to do because it could save your pooch's life. They are likely to lunge at things that look like food when you are out for a walk, and being so low to the ground, they are probably going to see a lot of food-like things long before you do. This command gets them to drop whatever they are munching on before ingesting it.

Quiet

In the beginning, you can also use treats sparingly to reinforce quiet. If your puppy is barking for no apparent reason, tell the puppy to be quiet and place a treat nearby. It is almost guaranteed that the dog will fall silent to sniff the treat, in which case, say good dog or good quiet. It will not take too long for your puppy to understand that quiet means no barking. However, it may take a while for your puppy to learn to fight the urge to bark. Be patient with your puppy because it is difficult to stop doing something that you do naturally. How long did it take you to learn to get up early in the morning or to go to bed at a certain time? It is similar for a Chihuahua to learn not to bark.

Where to Go from Here

These are all the commands that you are likely to need with your Chihuahua. However, if you want your Chihuahua to do tricks, you can pretty much go anywhere from here. These commands are the foundation of training, and the Chihuahua is capable of learning so much more. Just make sure that the tricks that you teach your Chihuahua are not too stressful for your puppy. As your puppy ages, you can start teaching tricks that highlight your puppy's agility. Fetch and other interactive tricks will be ideal because your Chihuahua will want to do them.

CHAPTER 14.
Nutrition

With a Chihuahua's healthy weight of around 6 pounds, you know that you cannot be giving your Chihuahua a lot of extra food. He cannot go run it off in the yard like a larger dog, and his little legs aren't going to take him on hour-long walks. The fact that he is easy to satisfy for his daily exercise is one reason why people often choose Chihuahuas as a pet. The problem is that with such a small package, it does not take much additional food to overfeed your little one.

His dietary needs are also a bit different from those of a lot of other breeds. According to Linda Jangula of Chihuahuas Wee Love, "The Chihuahua does not need as high of a protein diet as other breeds and of course low fat. Many enjoy a nibble of a fresh apple bite, a slice of raw carrot or even a bite of kale or collard stem to crunch on."

The reason these are suggested as treats is that they are low-calorie solutions to keeping your little pup healthy. Those little nibbles for snacks and Cheerios for training can help you keep your little Chihuahua healthy. Ensuring your Chihuahua gets the right nutritional balance is critical for a long, happy life.

Why a Healthy Diet Is Important

Chihuahuas are not a particularly energetic dog, which means that you have to be very careful to balance his eating habits with his exercise levels. Even though it takes a lot more energy for him or her to go the same distance on a walk, you won't have him out often enough to work off overeating or too many calories. Overfeeding your Chihuahua is incredibly easy because he does not need much food before he reaches his caloric needs for the day. Many of the tricks and activities that he does can expend a good bit of energy, but that does not mean that he needs a lot of food. If you have a very busy schedule, it will be entirely too easy to have substantial lapses in activity levels while you are home. Your Chihuahua is still going to expect the same amount of food, regardless of activity level. This means he is likely to start putting on weight, which will be detrimental to his health.

HELPFUL TIP
Avoid Obesity

Obesity causes the same health problems in Chihuahuas that it does in humans, and many Chihuahuas are overweight due to their owners overfeeding them. It may be that you're giving your Chihuahua too much kibble or too many treats. Either way, it's crucial to keep your Chihuahua at a healthy weight. You should be able to feel (but not see) its ribs without too much effort.

You need to not only be careful of how much you feed your Chihuahua during meal time, but how many treats you offer over the course of the day. All food needs to be considered when you consider both nutritional and caloric intake. Because of his tiny little body, you need to be aware of roughly how many calories your dog eats a day. If you notice that your dog is putting on weight, you will be able to adjust how much food he eats a day, or change the food to something with more nutritional value.

Breeders also recommend that you avoid food made of grains. Grains can make them gain weight faster. If you have the time, it is best to make your dog's meals – or at least provide real food mixed with their dog food.

In addition to their size, Chihuahuas tend to have very bad teeth. As Stephanie Lucas of Lucas Chihuahuas notes, "Giving a high quality dry food and marrow bones from puppy age will help." By being careful with their diet, you can help reduce the dental problems your Chihuahua will have.

Commercial Food

If you are one of the majority of puppy parents, make sure that you are buying the best dog food that you can find and afford. Take the time to research each of your options, particularly the nutritional value of the food. Always account for your dog's small stature, energy levels, and age. Your puppy may not need puppy food as much as other breeds (given the fact that he doesn't need nearly as many calories), and dog food for seniors may not be the best option for your senior Chihuahua. To provide more nutrition, you can mix some food into the processed food. This can help supplement any nutrients, as well as being a healthy addition to an otherwise entirely processed meal. The addition of a little bit of home-cooked food with each meal will make your Chihuahua excited to eat.

Preparing Your Food Naturally at Home

If you want to provide the healthiest meals possible, you should plan to spend an extra five to ten minutes in the kitchen per meal you prepare for your Chihuahua. If you regularly make your own food (from scratch, not with a microwave or boxed meal), it really doesn't take that much more time to provide an equally healthy meal for your little companion.

Keeping in mind the foods that your Chihuahua absolutely should not eat, you can mix some of the food you make for yourself in your Chihuahua's meal. Just make sure to add a bit more of what your Chihuahua needs to the puppy food bowl. Although you and your Chihuahua have distinctly different dietary needs, you can tailor your foods to include nutrients that your dog needs. It won't really take that much longer to tailor a meal for you and a slightly different version for your dog. Read through Chapter 5 to make sure that you never give your Chihuahua food that could be harmful or deadly.

Do not feed your Chihuahua from your plate. Split the food, placing your dog's meal into a bowl so that your canine understands that your food is just for you. The best home-cooked meals should be planned in advance so that your Chihuahua is getting the right nutritional balance.

Typically, 50% of your dog's food should be animal protein (fish, poultry, and organ meats). About 25% should be full of complex carbohydrates. The remaining 25% should be from fruits and vegetables, particularly foods like pumpkin, apples, bananas, and green beans. These provide additional flavors that your Chihuahua will likely love while making the little pup feel full faster so that overeating is reduced.

Puppy Food vs. People Food

It is true that a puppy needs more calories than an adult, and with his small size, a Chihuahua puppy does not need nearly as much as you may think he does to meet the caloric needs for his energy levels. If you are bringing a Chihuahua puppy into your home and know that you aren't going to have the time to cook, you should get food designed for puppies. This will ensure that your puppy gets the necessary calories for growth. Do not feed the puppy people food under the belief that you can switch to dog food later – because that is going to be virtually impossible to do. Once your Chihuahua becomes an adult, it is nearly impossible to convince your canine that those unappetizing pellets are food, particularly when your dog knows what the food on your plate tastes like. Do not set a precedence that will create significant problems for yourself later. If you feed your Chihuahua home-cooked puppy food, you are going to have to keep making food for your dog once the puppy stage is a memory.

It is best to make your puppy's food if you can. There really isn't going to be that much of a difference in the amount of food between the puppy and adults stages. Their little bodies have special needs, and the first few months are critical. If you can make your puppy's meals (and know that

Photo Courtesy of Elisha Jade Swanson

FUN FACT
Celebrity Pets

Chihuahuas are common pets among celebrities, having found homes with people like Adrian Brody, Scarlett Johansson, Ashton Kutcher, Cesar Millan, Christina Ricci, Demi Moore, George Lopez, Hilary Duff, Jayne Mansfield, Enrico Caruso, Jennifer Love Hewitt, Katharine McPhee, Lupe Velez, Madonna, Marilyn Monroe, Mickey Rourke, Anne Heche, Paula Abdul, Reese Witherspoon, Sandra Bullock, Billie Holiday, and Sharon Osbourne

you can keep it up when your Chihuahua is an adult), this will be a lot healthier for your dog.

If you find that you have to start buying commercial food, you will need to start slowly mixing it into your adult dog's meal. Do not be surprised if you find the pellets are uneaten for a while. It will be a difficult process convincing your dog that this is food, but if you mix it with other things (and know that you are always going to need to mix at least a little real food in with the commercial food), your dog will be more likely to start eating it since it will smell like real food.

Dieting, Exercise, and Obesity

Your Chihuahua is not going to diet the way you may choose to diet. This means you have to keep a regular eating schedule for your dog – his day is going to be based largely on the times of the day that are designated to eating. If treats and snacks are something you establish as normal early on, your dog is going to believe that is also a part of the routine and will expect it. Obviously, this can be a terrible habit to establish with your Chihuahua, especially if it is food that you are sharing because you are snacking and feel guilty. You will need to make sure to be active after snacking so that your Chihuahua doesn't get too many calories. An extra round of play or another walk can go a long way to helping keep your Chihuahua at a healthy weight.

There needs to be a healthy balance of diet and exercise to keep your Chihuahua from becoming overweight, certainly to avoid your dog becoming obese. Exercise is an absolute must. While you are helping your Chihuahua develop healthy eating and exercise habits, you are probably helping yourself. Being more aware of your dog's diet and exercise levels will probably make you more aware of your own. Obesity is something that you will need to actively avoid with a small dog. Get used to exercising and playing as a reward system.

Warning about Overfeeding and the Right Caloric Requirement

"Go easy on the treats or they can become obese easily. Healthy treats can be carrots, bananas, apples or treats like bully sticks, chicken feet or trachea."

Kathy Golden
Kactus Kathy's Chihuahuas

You have to be careful of your Chihuahua's weight, so you need to get used to monitoring it, particularly once your dog is an adult. Those snacks you share are not healthy, and your dog will pick up weight a lot faster than you will eating the same foods with less exercise. This is not really a reward for your Chihuahua – it's a hazard. Keep your dog on a diet that is healthy instead of indulging the little cutie. This will keep you both a lot happier in the long run.

Weighing your Chihuahua will be very helpful to ensuring that the pooch is staying at a healthy weight. Because he is really toy sized, you can use your own scales to weigh him. Gently pick up your canine and step on the scale. Subtract your weight from the total, and that is how much your Chihuahua weighs. Be honest about your weight. That means weighing yourself just before weighing your Chihuahua, and being accurate with the number. Counting calories is time consuming, but you should also know roughly how many calories your Chihuahua eats in a day because it really does not take much to meet the needs of such a small dog.

Obese Example

CHAPTER 15.
Grooming – Productive Bonding

Chihuahuas are incredibly healthy dogs as long as you keep in mind their limitations. Your puppy's size also makes it incredibly easy to groom him, although there are a few things you need to keep in mind as you take care of your pup's appearance. However, there is one area that will require regular attention, and that is his teeth. You will need to take care of the pup's teeth every day. Make it part of your daily grooming routine, and you won't have to worry too much about excess dog hair or foul breath.

The long-haired Chihuahuas are less prone to ear infections than most other small dogs. This certainly is a pleasant surprise for most people. As long as you take the necessary precautions you would with any other breed when it comes to water near their ears, your pup should be fine.

*Photo Courtesy of
Tasha Snitch*

Managing Your Chihuahua's Coat

Weekly, or even daily brushing, is the perfect way to bond with your puppy and to keep the relationship strong well into your pup's golden years. The regular attention will be something that your dog will look forward to as a part of the routine. It will also be a nice way to relieve stress since petting a dog is an easy way to help you calm down. That little body is going to be incredibly easy to brush every day – it probably won't take you 10 minutes. This makes it a quick and easy task that everyone can enjoy.

Puppy

As you can probably guess, brushing a puppy is going to take you more time. There will be a lot of wiggling and attempts at play. Trying to tell your puppy that the brush is not a toy clearly isn't going to work, so be prepared to be patient during each brushing session. On the other hand, your puppy is so adorable, you probably won't mind that it takes a bit longer.

You can plan to brush your puppy after vigorous exercise so that your Chihuahua has far less energy to fight or play. Be careful that you

FUN FACT
Short and Long Coats

Did you know that Chihuahuas with both short and long coats can be born to the same litter? That's because the long coat is a recessive gene rather than a separate breed type. Thanks to the recessive gene, two Chihuahuas with short coats can have a puppy with a long coat.

don't encourage rambunctious behavior during brushing because this will become part of the routine, and your Chihuahua will think that the brush is meant for playtime, and it is going to be difficult to convince him that it isn't true the longer it happens. Maybe you won't mind in the beginning, but there will be times when you just want to finish brushing your dog quickly, and that is why you need to make sure your puppy doesn't think it is time to play.

As you get accustomed to brushing your puppy, get accustomed to checking his skin. Look for rashes, sores, or infections. You should also check his ears, eyes, and mouth while you are grooming him. Keep doing these activities even after your Chihuahua is an adult. Since Chihuahuas have such small bodies, it won't be that time consuming, and it will help you to spot potential issues as early as possible.

Adulthood

Tangles are not something you have to worry about with Chihuahuas, but you do need to be careful of their skin. Brushing probably wouldn't take too long and you won't mind making it nearly a daily activity.

Baths should be a regular part of the schedule too, although it will vary based on the time of year. Another thing you need to clean regularly is the wrinkles on the face. These can trap dirt, making them potentially dangerous little areas that can become infected. This is a really quick activity, but you do need to be careful. Use a lightly damp cloth so that you don't make the folds of the wrinkles wet. Of course, you may not think of your Chihuahua as having a dirty face, but it is important to keep the folds clean.

Trimming the Nails

Because Chihuahuas have such small paws, you have to be very careful about trimming the nails. If you feel at all uncomfortable, you might want to have a professional trim your Chihuahua's nails. You can always study how it is done and learn how to do it yourself over time. While he is still a puppy though, your Chihuahua may be a little too enthusiastic for you to do the cutting.

The puppy's nails should be cut about once a week since your Chihuahua will probably be on concrete and asphalt less often than a larger dog. Without these hard surfaces to help keep the nails filed, regular grooming will be required to keep the nails from being too long.

Once your dog is an adult, check the nails monthly. As you will be walking him more often on sidewalks or other kinds of surfaces that will help keep his nails shorter, grooming can be done less frequently. It is possible that you won't need to trim them for months at a time if your Chihuahua walks on concrete or asphalt enough to keep his nails short. However, if you don't walk as much on these surfaces in the winter, you will need to increase how often you trim the nails.

Brushing Their Teeth

"Chihuahuas notoriously have bad teeth, tartar buildup, gum recession and missing teeth with mouth infection. It is vitally important that the teeth be brushed on a regular basis beginning as soon as you get your puppy home."

Barbara Pendergrass
Rafina Chihuahuas

Chihuahuas have notoriously bad teeth and gums. You are going to need to plan to take care of those little needles in your Chihuahua's mouth from day one, even though it means getting your hands up close.

Daily brushing of the teeth can be done before or after brushing your pup's coat. It is the perfect way to bond with your puppy and to keep the relationship strong well into your Chihuahua's golden years. The regular attention will be

Photo Courtesy of Crystal Jay Herrald-Campbell

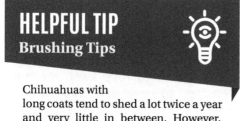

HELPFUL TIP
Brushing Tips

Chihuahuas with long coats tend to shed a lot twice a year and very little in between. However, they do still need weekly brushing with a slicker brush and a comb to prevent knots from forming in their coat. Short-haired Chihuahuas shed year-round and benefit from weekly brushing with a rubber curry-style brush.

something that your dog will look forward to as a part of the routine.

In case you think that it might be all right to let it go, here are a couple of warnings from breeders.

"They tend to lose their teeth...plan on getting dental care from the vet about every 3 or 4 years." - Stephanie Lucas of Lucas Chihuahuas

"Chihuahuas notoriously have bad teeth, tartar buildup, gum recession and missing teeth with mouth infection. It is vitally important that the teeth be brushed on a regular basis beginning as soon as you get your puppy home. I recommend brushing a minimum of 3 times a week...the brushing is going to be done to get him used to the process rather than with the goal of cleaning." - Barbara Pendergrass of Rafina Chihuahuas

Since Chihuahuas can live up to two decades, you want to keep their teeth as clean as possible. If you don't want to brush his teeth regularly, you can have your Chihuahua's teeth cleaned once a year for several hundred dollars.

If you opt to brush your pup's teeth, you already know that your Chihuahua will be all over you most of the time anyway. This constant close contact will give you a pretty good idea of when to brush his teeth – if you can't stand the smell emanating from your dog's mouth, stop what you are doing and brush those teeth. Regular brushing keeps the dog's teeth clean and healthy. If you notice that plaque and tartar are building up quickly, or that your dog's breath smells foul faster, you can increase how often you conduct the brushing ritual.

Cleaning Ears and Eyes

Check your dog's ears for build-up of wax, infection, or other potential problems. This is something that should be done for most breeds depending on how often you bathe them. If you get water in your Chihuahua's ears it can cause an infection, so monitoring for it is important.

Chihuahuas do not tend to have many problems with their eyes, despite the fact that the eyes take up a large percentage of their face. You should still check to make sure that your Chihuahua does not get dirt in them after an outdoor adventure. If it looks like dirt has gotten in your dog's eye or eyes, you can use an eye wash approved by your vet. Usually, if your dog's fur is coated in dirt, then you should check to make sure the dirt and mud did not get in your pup's eyes.

CHAPTER 16.
Basic Health Care

Chihuahuas can be great little companions with the right social-ization. That will be your primary focus because they are a pretty healthy little breed. Remember, this does not mean that they are sturdy. As long as you are careful and take good care of your little buddy, you will have 15 to 20 years to enjoy your exuberant little companion.

There are some basic preventative measures you should take to make sure your puppy stays healthy. Many of the treatments and con-cerns are universal across the entire canine world, which means there is a good chance you already know that you need to take care of your small dog. You can consider this chapter as more of a reminder or checklist of things you probably already know you need to be aware of. Treating and keeping your puppy free of parasites should be something that you add to your budget once they are old enough for the treatments.

Fleas and Ticks

Since Chihuahuas don't require much outdoor time, they are at a lower risk of getting ticks. Fleas are something that you will need to watch for since they live in yards too. Your little Chihuahua is going to be outside some of the time, which means you still have to monitor him. If your Chihuahua loves roaming through high grass, you cannot allow any lapse in treatment, even in winter.

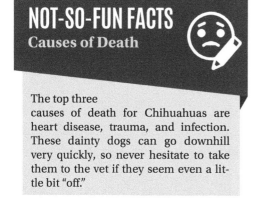

NOT-SO-FUN FACTS
Causes of Death

The top three causes of death for Chihuahuas are heart disease, trauma, and infection. These dainty dogs can go downhill very quickly, so never hesitate to take them to the vet if they seem even a lit-tle bit "off."

With each bath that you give your Chihuahua, make time to check for ticks and fleas as part of the cleaning process. Comb through the fur and check the skin for irritation and parasites. This will help keep your puppy healthier and feeling much bet-ter. Since you will be doing this often, you should be able to know when a bump is a prob-lem. Since your dog will be very happy to spend time with you, it shouldn't take as long as you think – it isn't as though you will have to spend a lot of time struggling to get your Chihuahua to sit still for a tick check.

Photo Courtesy of Teresa Forbes

Fleas will be more problematic because they are far more mobile. The best way to look for fleas is to make it a regular part of your brushing sessions. You can also look for behavioral indicators, such as incessant scratching and licking. With the regular checks on your pup's skin when brushing his or her hair, you will be able to check the spots where your dog is scratching to see if the skin is irritated or if it is the work of a flea. Given the small stature of your companion, fleas will have no trouble jumping on your Chihuahua from the grass or other vegetation. This means you will need to use flea preventative products on a regular basis. You won't be able to do this with puppies under a certain age, but once they mature, you can start adding the cost of treatment to the budget and schedule.

If you want to use natural products instead of the chemical-filled products, set aside a few hours to research the alternatives and find out what works best for your Chihuahua. Do not increase the number of baths because their skin is sensitive and should not be washed too often, so that should not be part of the solution. Do verify that any natural product purchases work before you buy them.

Remedies should be applied monthly. Establishing a regular schedule and adding it to the calendar will help you remember to treat your dog on schedule.

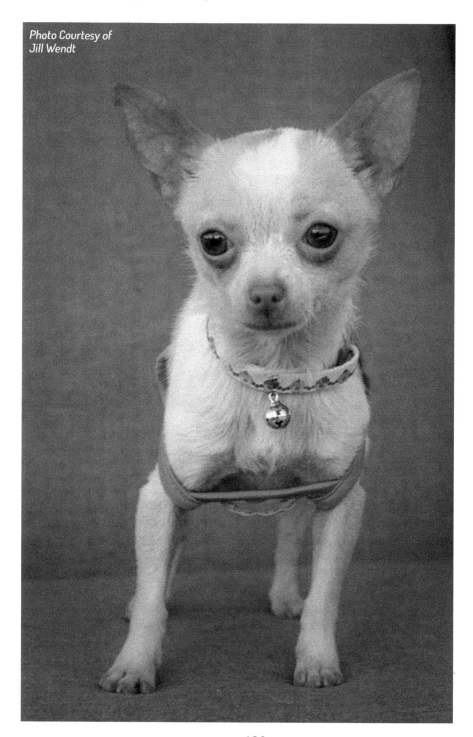

Photo Courtesy of
Jill Wendt

Worms and Parasites

Although worms and other types of parasites are a less common problem than fleas and ticks, they can be far more dangerous. There are a number of types of worms that you should be aware of:

- Heartworms

- Hookworms

- Roundworms

- Tapeworms

- Whipworms

One of the primary problems is that there isn't an easy to recognize set of symptoms to help identify when your dog has a problem with worms. However, you can keep an eye out for these symptoms, and if your dog shows them, you should schedule a visit to the vet.

- If your Chihuahua is unexpectedly lethargic for at least a few days.

- Patches of fur begin to fall out (this will be noticeable if you brush your Chihuahua regularly) or if you notice patchy spaces in your dog's coat.

- If your dog's stomach becomes distended (expands), set up an appointment immediately to have him or her checked. Your dog's stomach will look like a potbelly.
- Your Chihuahua begins coughing, vomiting, has diarrhea, or has a loss in appetite.

These symptoms should be more obvious in a Chihuahua because they tend to be active or with you all of the time. If you aren't sure, it is best to get to the vet as soon as possible to check for problems.

If your dog has hookworms or roundworms, you will also need to visit a doctor to get checked yourself. These worms can be spread to you from your dog through skin contact. If your dog has them, you are at risk of contracting them. Being treated at the same time can help stop the vicious cycle of continually switching which of you has worms.

Heartworms are a significant threat to your dog's health as they can be deadly. You should be actively treating your dog to ensure that this parasite does not have a home in your dog. There are medications that can ensure your Chihuahua does not get or have heartworms.

Benefits of Veterinarians

Your dog should have regular visits to your vet, just like you have regular checkups for yourself. From regular shots to healthy checkups, vets will make sure that your Chihuahua stays healthy. With a number of potential issues, you want to make sure that your Chihuahua doesn't have any of the many possible problems.

Since Chihuahuas are such eager companions, it is going to be obvious when they aren't acting normal. Annual visits to the vet will ensure there isn't a problem that is slowly draining the energy or health from your dog.

Health checkups also make sure that your Chihuahua is aging well. If there are any early symptoms of something potentially wrong with your dog over the years (such as arthritis), you will be able to start making adjustments. The vet can help you come up with ways to manage pain and problems that come with the aging process. Your vet will be able to recommend adjustments to the schedule to accommodate your canine's aging body and diminishing abilities. This will ensure that you can keep having fun together without hurting your dog. These changes are well worth it in the end because your dog will able to keep enjoying time with you without suffering additional pain.

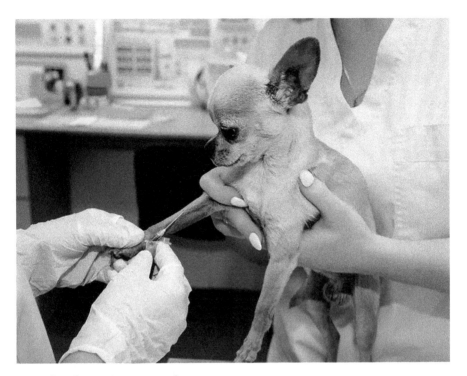

Holistic Alternatives

Wanting to keep a dog from a lot of exposure to chemical treatments makes sense, and there are many good reasons why people are moving to more holistic methods. However, doing this does require a lot more research and monitoring to ensure that the methods are working – and more importantly, that they do not harm your dog. Unverified holistic medicines can be a waste of money, or, worse, they can even be harmful to your pet. Other methods have often been used for far longer, so there is more data to ensure that they aren't doing more harm than good. However, natural methods that work are always preferable to any chemical solution.

If you decide to go with holistic medication, talk with your vet about your options. You can also seek out Chihuahua experts to see what they recommend before you start using any methods you are interested in trying. Read what scientists have said about the medicine. There is a chance that the products you buy from a store are actually better than some holistic medications.

Make sure you are thorough in your research and that you do not take any unnecessary risks with the health of your Chihuahua.

133

Photo Courtesy of
Carrie-Anne Selwyn

Vaccinating Your Chihuahua

Vaccination schedules are almost universal for all dog breeds, including Chihuahuas. Use the following to ensure that your Chihuahua receives the shots needed on time.

- The first shots are required at between 6 and 8 weeks following the birth of your Chihuahua. You should find out from the breeder if these shots have been taken care of and get the records of the shots:
  - Corona virus
  - Distemper
  - Hepatitis
  - Leptospirosis
  - Parainfluenza
  - Parvo
- These same shots are required again at between 10 and 12 weeks of age.
- These same shots are required again at between 14 and 15 weeks old, as well as his or her first rabies shot.
- Your dog will need to get these shots annually after that. Your Chihuahua will also need annual rabies shots.

Once you start the shots, you need to see them through to the end. Make sure to get the schedule for upkeep on these shots. Then you will need to maintain these shots over the years, particularly shots like rabies.

CHAPTER 17.
Health Concerns

Photo Courtesy of Emma Robertson

For the most part, Chihuahuas are incredibly healthy dogs, especially for their size. However, that size does make them far easier to accidentally hurt. Also, puppies from puppy mills and bad breeders are much more likely to have very serious health concerns. This is one very important reason to do your research into breeders before you buy a puppy.

Purebreds all have known issues, and dogs as a whole have some fairly predictable issues across all breeds. Ailments like hip dysplasia are common in most breeds, so you will need to keep an eye out for more than just the problems that most Chihuahuas can have or develop over time.

A Dog with Some Serious Health Concerns

Most Chihuahuas are incredibly healthy and will live to be 15 to 20 years old. That does not mean the breed does not have the potential to get some very serious illnesses. You will need to keep an eye on your Chihuahua and be far more diligent in ensuring that he gets the right diet than you would with other breeds. Overfeeding, pampering, and being too rough are all very easy to do with a Chihuahua. The reason you and your family need to be very careful is because it does not take many times doing something to make it a habit. And bad habits with your Chihuahua could be detrimental to your dog's health.

Typical Purebred Health Issues

Chihuahuas are somewhat unpredictable when it comes to health issues. There is a rather long list of potential problems, but most Chihuahuas tend to be healthy. This means that there is low risk, but that doesn't mean no risk. Keep a careful eye on your Chihuahua over the years so that you are more likely to notice any poten-

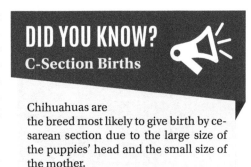

DID YOU KNOW?
C-Section Births

Chihuahuas are the breed most likely to give birth by cesarean section due to the large size of the puppies' head and the small size of the mother.

tial issues. The following are the problems of greatest concern:

- *Heart disease* – the best way to protect your Chihuahua from heart problems is to make sure that you don't let your dog get obese. Your dog's small frame cannot handle a lot of weight, and the strain it places on the heart is far more than the heart can handle for long periods of time.

- *Corneal Dystrophy* – As Chihuahuas age, a clear film can form over their eyelids. Some dogs won't notice it, while others can be severely impaired by the film. It is a problem that you will need to consult your vet about to find out the best answer for taking care of the problem.

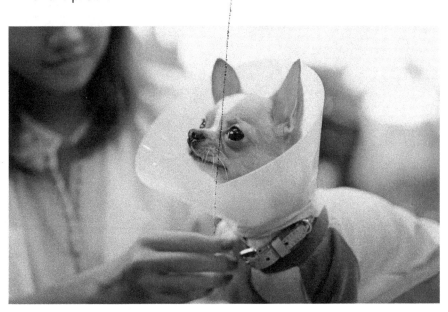

*Photo Courtesy of
Sarah Rihn*

- *Hydrocephalus* – This is a problem where fluid accumulates around the brain. Watch for your dog to be lethargic and uncoordinated to see some early symptoms. Seizures can be a more serious symptom, and your Chihuahua should be immediately taken to the vet. Be more aware of this problem if your Chihuahua has a particularly small head as well. It is possible for your Chihuahua to have the condition with minimal impact on your dog's life. However, it can also be fatal, so you should always monitor for it.

- *Tracheal collaps*e – Chihuahuas are prone to having this issue because of how weak their necks are. If you and your family are always gentle and careful when you leash your Chihuahua, it is unlikely to ever be a problem. This is one of the most important reasons why you cannot be rough with your Chihuahua. The extra pressure from pulling them along can cause long-term damage. Make sure the collar is not too tight as well. Ask your vet about possible supplements to help strengthen their necks. If you notice that your Chihuahua is having trouble breathing, especially if they have been very active, take your pup to the vet to be checked for this problem.

Where You Can Go Wrong

In addition to genetic problems, there are things that you can do that could damage your dog's health. These are related to the dog's diet and exercise levels. If you follow the recommendations in Chapter 16, your dog will remain healthy longer.

Importance of Breeder to Ensuring Health in Your Chihuahua

Being aware of the health of the parents and the diseases that are known to be a problem for them or their parents will help you know what to monitor for in your Chihuahua.

Any breeder that doesn't provide a health guarantee for a breed as established as the Chihuahua is not a breeder you should consider. Avoid all of these breeders – they are interested in the money, and the dog's health is of little to no concern. If a breeder says that a puppy or litter has to be kept in an isolated location for health reasons, do not work with that breeder.

Ask the breeder to talk about the history of the parents, the kinds of health problems that have been in the dog's family, and if the breeder has had problems with any particular illness in the past. If the breeder gives you only short or vague answers, this is a sign that the breeder has dogs that are more likely to have issues later.

Photo Courtesy of
Carrie-Anne Selwyn

Common Diseases and Conditions

Chihuahuas have problems with specific parts of their bodies. These are not the major health concerns covered above, but letting these problem go can result in serious problems later, as well as degrading your Chihuahua's life. The following are the areas where you need to monitor your Chihuahua:

- Dental hygiene
- Hip, shoulder, and knee dysplasia
- Urinary tract infections

Prevention & Monitoring

Beyond genetic issues (something you should learn about the parents before getting your puppy), the problem you have to worry about is weight. Previous chapters provide information about the right diet and exercise for your Chihuahua. Refraining from giving your Chihuahua foods made of grains and keeping their daily caloric intake within a healthy range area are essential given the dog's size. Considering the fact that they will eat whatever you give them, your dog's weight is always going to be a concern if you aren't careful. Your vet will likely talk to you if your dog has too much weight on his body because this not only puts a strain on the dog's legs, joints, and muscles, it can have adverse effects on your dog's heart, blood flow, and respiratory system.

HELPFUL TIP
Don't Forget the Teeth

Thanks to the small size of their mouths, Chihuahuas are prone to a lot of dental issues. Periodontal disease can even lead to heart failure if left untreated, so try to get in the habit of brushing your Chihuahua's teeth every day. Have the vet check your dog's teeth every year and get a dental cleaning any time your vet recommends it. Your Chihuahua's life could depend on it.

CHAPTER 18.
Your Aging Chihuahua

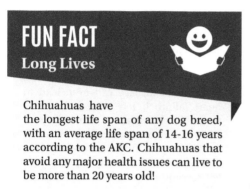

FUN FACT
Long Lives

Chihuahuas have the longest life span of any dog breed, with an average life span of 14-16 years according to the AKC. Chihuahuas that avoid any major health issues can live to be more than 20 years old!

Chihuahuas have a life expectancy of between 15 and 20 years. They are prone to some late in life problems, like one of a variety of different types of dysplasia, which will mean making some real changes in your life as your dog reaches the golden years. You will need to start making adjustments to accommodate his or her reduced abilities. A dog may remain healthy his or her entire life, but the body just won't be able to do the same activities at 12 that it could do at 2. The changes you need to make will be based on your Chihuahua's specific needs. The decline tends to be gradual, just little things here and there, like your Chihuahua having less traction on smooth surfaces. Over time, the body will start to deteriorate so that your dog will not be able to jump as high. One of the best ways to combat this is to have steps and other means of assisting your Chihuahua onto furniture from the time they are puppies. This reduces the amount of force on their limbs when jumping down, as well as making it easier for him to get up to you.

As your Chihuahua's energy and abilities decrease, you need to make sure that he or she is not overdoing it. You should always make sure your dog doesn't over-exercise, but this is even more important for an older dog. Chihuahuas may be too focused on having fun to realize they are hurting until they start to rest. These later years will be just as much fun; you will just need to make sure your Chihuahua isn't pushing the new limitations. It is easy to make the senior years incredibly enjoyable for your Chihuahua and yourself by making the necessary adjustments that allow your dog to keep being active without overexertion.

Senior Dog Care

It is usually easier to take care of a senior dog than a young dog, and the Chihuahua is no exception. Naps are just as exciting as walks. Sleeping beside you while you watch television or even if you nap with your dog is pretty much all it takes to make your Chihuahua happy (though that was probably true when they were young too).

However, you must continue to be vigilant about diet and exercise. Now is not the time to let your Chihuahua start to eat anything and everything or neglect to take your regular walks. A senior Chihuahua cannot handle extra weight, so you must be careful to ensure he or she remains healthy with age.

If your canine cannot manage long walks, make the walks shorter and more numerous and spend more time romping around your yard or home.

When it comes to items that your Chihuahua will need to access regularly, you should make some changes to your current configuration.

- Set water bowls out in a couple of different places so that your dog can easily reach them as needed. If your Chihuahua shows signs of having trouble drinking or eating, you can place water dishes around the home to make it easier for him or her to drink.

- Cover hard floor surfaces (such as tiles, hardwood, and vinyl). Use carpets or rugs that will not slip out from under your Chihuahua.

- Add cushions and softer bedding for your Chihuahua. This will both make the surface more comfortable and help your Chihuahua stay warmer. There are some bed warmers for dogs if your Chihuahua displays achy joints or muscles often. Of course, you also need to make sure your Chihuahua isn't too warm, so this can be a fine balancing act.

- Increase how often you brush your Chihuahua to improve his or her circulation. This should be very agreeable to your Chihuahua as a way to make up for other limitations that mean you can do other activities less often.

- Stay inside in extreme heat and cold. Your Chihuahua is hardy, but the old canine body cannot handle the extreme changes as well as once it did.

- Use stairs or ramps for your Chihuahua instead of constantly picking up your canine. Picking your Chihuahua up may be more convenient for you, but it is not healthy for you or your Chihuahua. Let your dog maintain a bit more self-sufficiency.

- Avoid changing your furniture around, particularly if your Chihuahua shows signs of having trouble with his or her sight. A familiar home is more comforting and less stressful as your pet ages. If your Chihuahua is not able to see as clearly as he or she once did, keeping the home familiar will make it easier for your dog to move around without getting hurt.

- If you have stairs, consider setting up an area where your dog can stay without having to use the stairs as often.

- Create a space where your Chihuahua can relax with fewer distractions and noises. Your Chihuahua will probably be even less comfortable being left alone for extended periods, but you should have a place where you and your older dog can just relax without loud or startling noises. Don't make your little friend feel isolated, but do give him or her a place to get away from everyone if he needs to be alone.

Nutrition

Since a decrease in exercise is inevitable for any aging dog, you will need to adjust your pet's diet. If you opt to feed your Chihuahua commercial dog food, make sure you change to the senior food. If you make your Chihuahua's food, take the time to research how best to reduce calories without sacrificing taste. Your canine is going to need less fat in his or her food, so you may need to find something healthier that still has a lot of taste to supplement the types of foods you gave your Chihuahua as a puppy or active adult dog.

Exercise

Exercise will be entirely up to you because your Chihuahua is still just happy to be with you. If you make fewer demands, decrease the number of walks, or in any way change the routine, your Chihuahua will quickly adapt to the new program. It is up to you to adjust the schedule and keep your Chihuahua happily active. Usually increasing the number of walks with shorter durations will help keep your Chihuahua as active as necessary.

Keep in mind that your Chihuahua is more likely to gain weight in the later years, something that his or her body really cannot handle. While the exercise will be reduced, it should not be eliminated. Keep to what your dog can manage and adjust food accordingly to keep the weight healthy.

This will probably be the hardest part of watching your Chihuahua age. However, you will need to watch your Chihuahua for signs of tiredness or pain so that you can stop exercising before your dog has done too much. Your pace will need to be slower and your attention more on your dog, but ultimately it can be just as exciting. You will probably notice that your Chihuahua spends more time sniffing. This could be a sign that your dog is tiring, or it could be his or her way of acknowledging that long steady walks are a thing of the past and is stopping to enjoy the little things more. It is an interesting time and gives you a chance to get to understand your Chihuahua as the years start to show. Your Chihuahua may also let you know that it is time to go home by turning around to go back or sitting down a lot and looking at you. Take the hint and go home if your Chihuahua lets you know that the limits have been reached.

Mental Stimulation

Unlike the body, your Chihuahua's mind is usually going to be just as sharp and clever in the golden years. That means you can start making adjustments to focus more on the activities that are mentally stimulating. You can start doing training for fun because your Chihuahua will be just as able to learn now as when he or she was 1 year old. Actually, it is likely to be easier because your Chihuahua has learned to focus better and the bond will make him happy to have something he can still do with you.

Your Chihuahua will be grateful for the shift in focus and additional attention. Getting your senior Chihuahua new toys is one way to help keep your dog's mind active if you do not want to train your dog or if you just don't have the time. You can then teach the Chihuahua different names for the toys because it will be fascinating (after all, he or she will still work for praise). Whatever toys you get, make sure they are not too rough on your dog's older jaw and teeth. Tug of war may be a game of the past (you don't want to hurt the old teeth), but other games are still very much appreciated.

Hide and seek is another game that your aging Chihuahua can manage with relative ease. Whether you hide toys or yourself, this can be a game that keeps your Chihuahua guessing.

Regular Vet Exams

Just as humans go to visit the doctor more often as they age, you are going to need to take your dog to see your vet with greater frequency. The vet can make sure that your Chihuahua is staying active without being too active, and that there is no unnecessary stress on your older dog. If your canine has sustained an injury and hidden it from you, your vet is more likely to detect it.

Your vet can also make recommendations about activities and changes to your schedule based on your Chihuahua's physical abilities and any changes in personality. For example, if your Chihuahua is panting more now, it could be a sign of pain from stiffness. This could be difficult to distinguish given how much Chihuahuas pant as a rule, but if you see other signs of pain, schedule a visit with the vet. Your vet can help you determine the best way to keep your Chihuahua happy and active during the later years.

Common Old-age Ailments

Chapters 4 and 17 cover the illnesses that are common or likely with a Chihuahua, but old age tends to bring a slew of ailments that are not particular to any one breed. Here are the things you will need to watch for (as well as talking to your vet about them).

- Diabetes is probably the greatest concern for a breed that loves to eat as much as your Chihuahua does, especially because he has such a small frame. Although it is usually thought of as a genetic condition, any Chihuahua can become diabetic if not fed and exercised properly. It is another reason why it is so important to be careful with your Chihuahua's diet and exercise levels.

- Arthritis is probably the most common ailment in any dog breed, and the Chihuahua is no exception. If your dog is showing signs of stiffness and pain after normal activities, it is very likely that he or she has arthritis. Talk with your vet about safe ways to help minimize the pain and discomfort of this common joint ailment.

- Gum disease is a common issue in older dogs as well, and you should be just as vigilant about brushing teeth when your dog gets older as you do at any other age. A regular check on your Chihuahua's teeth and gums can help ensure this is not a problem.

- Loss of eyesight or blindness is relatively common in older dogs, just as it is in humans. Unlike humans, however, dogs don't do well with wearing glasses. Have your dog's vision checked at least once a year and more often if it is obvious that his or her eyesight is failing. Those large eyes will need extra attention.

- Kidney disease is a common problem in older dogs, and one that you should monitor for the older your Chihuahua gets. If your canine is drinking more often and having accidents regularly, this could be a sign of something more serious than just aging. If you notice this happening, get your Chihuahua to the vet as soon as possible and have him or her checked for kidney disease.

Enjoying the Final Years

The last years of your Chihuahua's life can actually be just as enjoyable (if not more so) than earlier stages. The energy and activities that the two of you used to do will be replaced with more attention and relaxation than at any other time. Finally having your Chihuahua be calm enough to just sit still and enjoy your company can be incredibly nice (just

remember to keep up his or her activity levels instead of getting too complacent with your Chihuahua's newfound love of resting and relaxing).

Steps and Ramps

Chihuahuas are small, but that does not mean that you should be picking them up more often as they age. Picking up your dog more often can even do more physical harm. There are two good reasons to ensure your Chihuahua is able to move around without you picking him or her up.

- Having an older body means they are fragile and should not be picked up to avoid unnecessary pain.
- Independence in movement is best for you and your Chihuahua. You do not want your Chihuahua to come to expect you to pick him or her up every time he or she wants to get on the furniture or into the car.

Steps and ramps are the best way to ensure your Chihuahua can keep some level of self-sufficiency. Also, you don't want to spoil your Chihuahua in the later years. Using steps and ramps provides a bit of different activity that can work as a way of getting a bit of extra exercise.

Enjoy the Advantages

A Chihuahua can be just as much fun in old age because his or her favorite thing is being with you. Your pet is just as mischievous as during the early years, but has learned to chill a bit more.

Your pet will find the warmest and most comfortable places, and will want you to join him or her. Your dog is incredibly devoted and will be happy to just share a short stroll followed by a lazy evening at home.

What to Expect

Your Chihuahua probably isn't going to suffer from fear that you are less interested in spending time together. He or she will continue be the loving mischief maker at every opportunity – that does not change with age. Just how much they can do changes. Your canine's limitations should dictate interactions and activities. If you are busy, make sure you schedule time with your Chihuahua to do things that are within those limitations. Your happiness is still of utmost importance to your dog, so let the little canine know you feel the same way about his or her happiness. It is just as easy to make an older Chihuahua happy as it is a young one, and it is easier on you since relaxing is more essential.

Ingram Content Group UK Ltd.
Milton Keynes UK
UKHW020625200423
420485UK00001B/35